FAIRACRES PUBLICATIONS 236

INSTRUMENTS OF THE PASSION

Lucy McKitterick

Fairacres Publications 236

ISBN 978-0-7283-0190-0
Fairacres Publications Series ISSN 0307-1405

Edited and typeset in Palatino Linotype by Julia Craig-McFeely

Cover image
Jean-Bernard Lalanne, 'Simon de Cyrène' reproduced by
kind permission of the artist.

SLG Press
Convent of the Incarnation
Fairacres • Oxford
www.slgpress.co.uk

Printed by
Grosvenor Group Ltd, Loughton, Essex

CONTENTS

*Jesus by thy cup of tears
awaken my heart to thy will.
Jesus by the lantern that sought thee
illumine the night of my fear.
Jesus by the ropes that bound thee
compel me to follow the way.
Jesus by the cock that crowed for thee
pardon all my denials.*

*Jesus by the pillar where they led thee
help me to seek thy mercy.
Jesus by the scourge that rent thee
chasten my disobedience.
Jesus by the thorns that crowned thee
prick my worldly pride.
Jesus by the hands that were washed of thee
do not abandon my soul.*

*Jesus by thy holy cross
help me to take up mine.
Jesus by the robe they stripped from thee
unclothe all my pretence.
Jesus by the dice they threw for thee
spare me the lot I have earned.
Jesus by the script that condemned thee
help me confess my sin.*

INSTRUMENTS
OF THE
PASSION

1

THE CUP

It was in the garden that I first met Stephen. It was late on an autumn evening, long since dark, coming on to rain. I had checked through the log from the late shift and handed over to the next team, and the doorbell rang again. 'I'll go.' I looked out into the night.

I could see the autumn trees damp with falling leaves in the neon lighting over the park, a mist was rising. The traffic on the road above had gone and the garden was quiet, wet grass, dark hedge, some plates and mugs left on the gravel. Jacob had his arm around his father, holding him up. 'Where are you staying?' I asked. We had just the one vacant bed.

We had seen a father and son before, the older man leading, the younger just out of prison. They had sat side by side at the dinner table, stayed some weeks before the younger jumped from an upstairs window one morning to evade the police and I said we couldn't have him back. But Jacob was different. 'My Dad needs help.' I brought a kitchen chair outside. Stephen wouldn't sit on it. 'For Christ's sake Dad you need to sit down.' Where were they staying? Nowhere, the foyer of a block of flats, outside sometimes, wherever. Stephen wouldn't look at me.

I visited Jerusalem as a pilgrim, nothing more, on holiday and with no special claim to historical or archaeological expertise. I found an uneasy city, where the Palestinian café by the Fourth

Station of the Cross served falafel under the gaze of armed teenage Israeli soldiers across the road. I watched Jewish schoolgirls in black school uniforms buying sweets on the way to class, and Arab grandmothers squatting in shawls begging shekels for bread. I walked for the first time where Jesus had walked, and began to understand why pilgrims call the land the 'fifth Gospel', and urge others to go. After I came home I went one day to Mass and found myself looking at a series of paintings over the chancel arch, the objects which marked the last hours of his life. The cup, the Crown of Thorns, the Cross, the tomb … pictures done in black and red. I looked and began to wonder what these things might look like at home.

The instruments of the Passion. The things which he uses to conquer the hurt and wrong of this world, the weapons we turn against him but which he takes for himself to battle the things which hurt and threaten us. Jesus asked his disciples, 'Can you drink the cup that I am about to drink?' And without knowing what was in it they answered, 'We can.' Then they fell asleep in the garden. But in the lonely moonlight Jesus is taking the cup, and all that we have put inside.

They slept. And such is the love of Jesus for us that he will fight while we sleep, in our sleep of ignorance, of negligence, of pride and self-will, of coldness of heart. He will fight for us with mercy and forgiveness, with patient waiting for the time to come when something in this world or the next wakens us to what he is doing. He will stand on the lake shore and wait, and ask us 'do you love me' not because he needs to hear the answer but because he knows we need to say it. He will do this, and yet he does not want us to delay. He invites us, here and now, to find the instruments of the Passion in our own place and time and to join the battle for our souls. 'Watch with me while I pray.'

✦

I talked with Jacob. His father was sick, he said, he had a bad leg. 'What kind of bad?' I said to Stephen, looking at the stained jeans, a lip of dirty bandage just visible below. No answer. Could Jacob have a cup of tea? 'Of course,' I said, 'how about you Stephen?' 'No I don't need anything.' I got a cup of tea, three sugars, and two referral forms. 'Okay let's start with Stephen. What's your date of birth — great — do you know your National Insurance number? — wonderful — when did you last have a home? 2008, I'm so sorry, that is a long time to be homeless. What happened?' We always asked the same questions. Such invasive questions, really, for anyone to be expected to answer for a stranger's risk assessment. I was amazed by people's honesty, standing there on the doorstep, at the responses they gave to 'Do you have a criminal record … what was that for, are you using street drugs, are you alcohol dependent,' trying to keep my voice impartial, gently concerned, thinking how they must be feeling, 'Have you been made to work without being paid … or been abused?' We made a point of taking everything they told us at face value. And of being ready, later, to listen and to write down something else.

He answered, cautiously, his son helping him out. They told me how Jacob's mother had died, how Stephen, broken by the loss, had been unable to keep up payments on the house. How they had gone to live with Stephen's parents, how he had tried to be a father to Jacob and his sister, how cocaine and heroin had taken him away. 'We have a room here,' I said, looking at Jacob. 'Dad, you take it.' But Stephen shook his head. He couldn't come in anywhere, he said, with his leg. It stank, he said. He was ashamed. 'Do you need to go to hospital?' I said, thinking of sepsis, gangrene. He followed my thought, 'No, I've not been for three months, I'm scared, they'll take my leg off.' He started to weep. 'I'm sure I've seen worse,' I said. He kept on shaking his head. 'Why don't we put some clean bandages on and see how you feel.' I went to fetch gloves, first-aid kit, sterile dressings, another plastic apron to serve as a mat. How inadequate these things are when people need a hospital—and how glad I was to have them when they will accept nothing else. When I came back Stephen was sitting on the kitchen chair, the cup of tea in his hands, and Jacob had his arm around him.

I had seen worse—just. I soaked and peeled, one-handed, the other in Stephen's, 'Just squeeze if I'm going too fast.' He sobbed, his face turned away, his son's arms around him. I talked to Jacob. 'What will you do?' I asked, 'we only have the one room.' 'I'll be fine,' he said, 'there's a mate I can stay with, but I couldn't leave Dad.' 'We'll keep your details too,' I said, 'we should have another room soon.' Jacob set to work to persuade his father to stay. 'You need help Dad. You need to accept it.' I finished the leg. 'Honestly you're not going to lose this,' I said, praying it was true, 'you just need to look after it, come and stay where you can rest and keep clean, it will be ok.' He sipped his tea, spilling some. I steadied his hand. 'Do you really think so?' 'Of course,' I said, 'and there's spag bol for dinner, would you like some?' He looked me in the eye for the first time, and saw that this at least he could believe. He tipped the mug back, and drained it. 'God yes!' he said, getting to his feet. And he followed me into the house.

✦

2

THE LANTERN

I found her curled up on the doorstep under the porch light, when I came in one morning for the early shift. It was still dark in the garden and I thought at first I was looking at a bundle of blankets, returned by someone we'd had to turn away and who had slept on a bench and woken early with the cold. Then I recognized her, rough brown hair, leopard print coat, a little dog in a child's pushchair whining gently. She had come the previous evening to sit on the step under the light, she said she felt safe. And she was still there.

We knew her slightly, the young lady with the confusing stories, who always seemed to be afraid of something, with the funny name she spelt for me a second time after I forgot, M-i-l-e-e. I had called the police with her once when she'd asked me to, only to find them frustrated and even more confused than me. I was dimly aware she had somewhere to live on the estate by the old railway line. Perhaps something was wrong at home.

We sat on the doorstep while she drank hot coffee. I listened and thought. We had a vacancy again—before the busy winter made it almost unknown for a room to be vacant overnight—but Milee had somewhere to stay, she had a tenancy, only she was saying she could not go back. I thought of the waiting list we had, people who were my next task of the morning to try and contact, people who had nowhere to go at all. 'What has happened at home?' I asked.

✦

The garden of Gethsemane is a little place now, a neat foursquare of ancient olives with a path for visitors around the edge. It is busy in the midday sun, with priests and pilgrims coming and looking and passing on. The stones are white in the sunlight, the rosemary sweet in the heat of the day. But if you go in the early morning all is quiet, and grey; you come there from the city, out through the wall and down and up again, the Mount of Olives rising black against the sky ahead and the road leading this way to the tombs of the prophets, that way to Gethsemane. The wadi Kidron, the valley of darkness, has a Jewish cemetery on the east side, a Muslim one on the west. Already, we are in a graveyard.

Was Jesus afraid, that night in the garden, when he saw them coming with lanterns? Or had fear left him, when he said to his Father, 'Thy will be done,' and went back to wake his disciples? Perhaps the cup of suffering answers that question, the cup of our own suffering and fear. He drank it, and everything that was in it, including the Christ-like courage of stepping forward even when we are afraid.

They came to seek him, through that valley of darkness, 'with lanterns and torches and weapons'. But the lantern which seeks us is the light of Christ, coming to find us, even when we think it is we who are searching for him. The Passion which begins with lights coming through the gnarled olive trees, with the be-trayer's kiss, will end on Easter night—as the Paschal candle is lit, and carried into church, and Jesus himself is the light who leads us on to the Easter feast. It is dark now, and we are afraid. And yet in our uncertainty, our fear of the future, we can know that we are in Gethsemane with him.

I had known that Milee earned money for sex. She had once mentioned the name of someone who had taken more than he paid for and added in a hoarse whisper, 'Tell the other working girls.' I didn't know I knew any others to tell, then, though as so often that was only my ignorance and some of the greatest cruelties in our communities are hidden in plain sight. I had realized that we saw her most often on Friday or Saturday evenings, made up, oddly focussed—we were, quite literally, her tea break, her safe space, her brief respite from the streets outside the town's club scene. The light in the porch was always on, and she came to it.

But that dim electric bulb, that damp doorstep, were so inadequate. Milee did have a tenancy, yes. She had left it some time in the summer—'you remember when you saw me in the café and I was four months pregnant? Well it was after that, I lost it, down the toilet at the flat, I'm not going back'—and had stayed first with Harry, then with her Dad. Harry had offered her crack for sex, she said, matter of fact as the cold morning air. Then he brought some mates home, more sex, same amount of drugs. Then he said she'd have to pay him too. So she got out through a window and went to her Dad's.

I didn't ask why she couldn't stay there. 'He knows where I live,' was all she would say. The trauma she had been through at home was terrible enough—but other women lose a stillborn child and don't leave to work as slaves for pimps and sleep rough on doorsteps. The greatest risk to Milee seemed to be something else I did not know. I thought again of our waiting list, she was not the only one to have slept outside that night. But Milee was here, and needing us—here, because we had cared for her, because we knew her name, because in all the chaos and pain of her existence she was frightened, and there was a light which was always on. 'What's the dog's name?' I asked, helping her inside, blankets trailing. She looked at me and grinned. 'It's Lucy!'

✦

3

THE ROPES

The system of drug dealing known as county lines is a complex web whose success lies in ensnaring the vulnerable and preying on the pain of others for money, and those who profit most will likely never meet those who suffer as a result. We rarely saw more than the consequences in our work—the ease of obtaining crack or heroin, the sickness and suffering which resulted—but now and again, in caring for them, someone would reveal a part of the hideous mechanics, the systems which police, in one campaign after another, worked to unpick. It was generally someone young, or without family, someone who'd grown up in care, weak among their peers and without the social capital which can give a person the confidence to protect themselves. They—whoever 'they' were—knew their victims well. And with us, that year, it was Frank.

He was a bright man, an answer for everything, keen to please. He was nearly thirty but like so many of the people we helped he was child-like, a cheeky thirteen-year-old wanting to be liked by his teachers rather than an adult who needed help to find a home. He had friends, when he had money in his pocket, and when he didn't they left him behind. It was among the outcasts from that outcast society, the ones nobody really wanted to know, that we saw him most often. They would gather on the benches outside the railway station, newly placed by the council as an arty public amenity and rapidly becoming the pub benches for people who could not afford to drink in a pub and would not have been welcome if they did.

And before long, people began to whisper. Someone had seen someone in town, making contacts: someone who'd got off a train from London, or perhaps a rail replacement bus, that conveniently less-supervised service with no transport police. Someone was approaching people on those benches — people who needed money for their own addictions and knew other people with needs too — and giving out drugs: a bag to keep if you sold nine and provided the mobile numbers and cash of the other victims. A change came over some of the people we knew: they were absent more, harder to talk to, barely around except to go to bed. And one night Frank was drunk and told us he had supplied crack to Milee, and he stood over her in the living room, shouting, demanding the money. Our first care had to be for the new child we now knew she was carrying, and we sent Frank away in the morning.

✛

They bound Jesus, there on the Mount of Olives where Judas had betrayed him, and they took him to the house of Caiaphas the high priest. You can visit the site today — as far as we can know it — and what might strike you first is how far they had to go, and how most of the way is steeply uphill. The place is on the slope on the south side of the city where the moon rising high in the sky shines on the rocks, above the pool of Siloam, where the valleys of darkness and Gehenna meet, where the man blind from birth was once healed. There is a church, and below it a crypt whose floor was very likely the courtyard of Caiaphas's house, and below that a prison hollowed out of the rock, and a pit. There were some hours yet to pass before they took Jesus on again and perhaps he passed the night, or part of it, down there. The pit has no stairs; a person could only be put in and lifted out on ropes. The prison is a cave, with two holes in the rock of the ceiling where a prisoner could be fastened up by the hands and flogged. It is a Jewish prison, a place for the punishment of one's own people, not a Roman one. The whole place is so vividly stamped with pain that if prison guards from two thousand years ago were to come down the steps you would not be surprised or think they were ghosts.

Jesus, by the light of a lantern under the olive trees, knowing both that place and the places which were to follow, allowed his captors to bind him. And we might picture the prison ourselves and reflect that this binding was a part of what lay in the cup of Gethsemane, the cup of obedience to the love which said 'Thy will be done,' and the beginning of the unbinding of the chains of human sin which disobedience to love has bound around us.

'When Israel was a child I loved him,' wrote the prophet Hosea, 'I led them with the cords of compassion, with the bindings of love.' To Jesus we are always children, if we will allow ourselves to be: not children in the sense of adults damaged by others who have not learned to grow up, nor compelled against our will, but children in our trust of God and in our certainty that we are loved and that what is given us can only be for our good. And we can have that certainty of goodness, because Jesus, in his love for us, has already bound himself to his people. The prison and the pit are ours, where on a moonlit night he allowed himself to be led up a stony hillside, and where sheer compassion is enough to lift us from the darkness into perfect safety. 'The Lord drew me up from the desolate pit,' wrote the Psalmist, 'out of the mire and clay.' Our God binds himself to us, and in doing so binds us to him.

They called him Matty, when they called him anything, and perhaps when we are with God it will seem less strange that in our frailty we should be called after the saints. It was Holy Week when the trouble over county lines seemed to come to a head, and Matty was mixed up in it, and when I asked Frank to leave us they would come to the door together, asking for food.

They must have been desperate, because after turning him out of the house I was surely the last person Frank wanted to see, and I had no kindness for Matty after I'd come across him the previous summer making love to one of the women we looked after, an overweight older man going up and down on a fragile girl in a field where they thought no one would see. I had been out on a walk as relief from emails, and found them in the long golden grass under a blue summer sky, and had been revolted. He came to the door when others were there to do the asking, and hung back against the wall, pushing the bits of food we gave him into his mouth in silence and going off into the night.

Yet I generally spent as much time as I could with the people who came to our door, standing among their chaos and their need and trying to understand. It was a part of the work that I loved, and I was impatient when a local residents' group in the town started a campaign of complaint; I never minded the drunkenness, or the noise sometimes, or the occasional visits from police cars—especially as most of those visits were to bring people home. And perhaps I thought of myself as a generous person, unfazed by the stories I heard; I listened in church from time to time to the parable of the sheep and goats and 'Lord when did we see you hungry, or thirsty, or naked, or in prison' and it didn't trouble me; 'Of course,' I thought, 'I can do that.' It is easy to do as we're asked, if it's what we wanted to do anyway. But there was a reason Matty didn't speak to me when he came for food. I had told the other staff what I had seen, and perhaps they were kinder than I was, but for me the revulsion came first, and he knew it.

And then there is Jesus in the garden, allowing himself to be bound with cords, and taken to that terrible place. If we allow ourselves to think a moment we will realize that the cords of compassion will not always seem like compassion to us, because they ask so much of us—not only our obedience to love when it suits us, but our perfect obedience when we are afraid to give it, as Jesus in Gethsemane gave his. County lines, and the consequences of them, made Frank once again homeless on the street. And the webs we are caught in can be frighteningly similar, where circumstances we cannot control, our weaknesses, our past, the cruelty of others, become entangled in our own words and actions until the little things we are tempted in grow greater and we are going our own way almost without seeing that we are. Jesus on the steep dark hillside shows us in the cold moonlight the ropes on his own hands, and in that binding offers us a way out.

✦

4

THE COCK THAT CROWED

It was the third winter that Patrick had stayed with us, and the first without Rachel. We had known them first as a couple, always fighting; they would come in together from the street in the evening, both drunk, Rachel often in tears. On one awful evening he'd thrown a plate at her head and I'd got him out of her room and held the door closed until the police came. It was a panelled door with a window, and he had smashed his head through the glass to carry on shouting more effectively.

I went to see Patrick in prison while he was on remand. It took some ingenuity to get there: not knowing his prisoner number, I could not call him or write to him, nor ask him to add me to his visitors list, so could not book a social visit as I had for others in prison before. They were sorry, the prison officer said on the phone, there was nothing they could do. After some thought I called them back. 'Could I book a legal visit please?' I asked, trying to sound like a solicitor with a lot of other jobs to fit in. I turned up on the allocated day, wondering if I might be stopped among the suits and buckle shoes, the people stowing laptops in the lockers. I took off the old coat which had seemed smart for work the day before, with the book I'd brought in case we had to wait, and I was led upstairs to a little grey room with a table and two chairs where I looked out between the window bars and thought I had never seen so bleak a place. The green of some weeds straggling by the razor-wire fence seemed indecently bright among the grey walls, grey concrete, grey sky.

Patrick, when he was shown in, wore a grey prison-issue track-suit. Somehow I'd never thought that prisoners in England, in some prisons, might still in the twenty-first century be in uniform. Even his face seemed grey.

We talked a bit, across the table. Something seemed wrong. I wondered if he was disappointed, if he'd hoped for a more useful visitor, if he didn't want to see someone who reminded him of what had brought him here. The allocated forty minutes seemed an impossible time to fill. 'Is everything ok?' I asked at last, in the silence, with only five minutes to go. He scraped a trainer with no laces on the grey lino floor. 'It's just … they said I had a legal visit. Is a solicitor coming here? I've only had the duty one at court before, it must be bad … how long am I going to get?' How stupid I had been not to have explained. 'I am the legal visit,' I said, 'it was the only way any of us could come,' and as it dawned on him that I was there for no purpose other than to show him that we cared about him, with an officer waiting at the door to return him to his cell he reached out over the table to pull me into a hug.

✦

The church built over the high priest Caiaphas's courtyard is called *in Gallicantu*, that is, 'where the cock crowed'. The crypt chapel, where you can see the old courtyard floor, has three huge icons on the walls—the denial of Peter on the left, with the maidservant, the fire, and Jesus turning and looking; the lakeside on the right, with Peter standing before his risen Lord; and in the middle, huge over the altar, Peter alone, his head in his hands. 'He went out and wept bitterly.'

An ancient tradition tells us that the lines drawn by the tears on Peter's face marked him for the rest of his life. And yet, standing in that place, knowing now as Peter would have done of the terrible prison below, we come nearer perhaps than in any place on the way to Calvary to understanding what that night would have felt like. Peter loved Jesus, he had leapt to defend him only hours before and attacked the high priest's servant with a sword. But in that courtyard, in the coldest hour of the night, alone among strangers and knowing of the prison and pit below, he must have been terrified. 'The Lord turned and looked at Peter.' And Peter's heart broke with grief and guilt and despair.

But it is this picture—Peter alone, weeping—which takes the central place over the altar, not his restoration, nor even his betrayal. The tears making lines on his face are to mark us too as we think of it, to change us as they changed everything for Peter because they changed how he stood with his Lord. 'The tax collector stood at the back of the temple and beat his breast … and I tell you, that man went home justified.' We must pray for the grace to weep like that. We must pray, because the crowing of the cock came not to taunt him, but to waken Peter and all of us to learn repentance, and so to find that it is morning and that in our grief we are with God.

✦

Patrick served his time in prison. And when he came out Rachel was already too familiar with hospital, because she had been diagnosed with breast cancer, and one breast had already gone. She was staying with a friend, using heroin again, which he hated her doing, and one morning she became rapidly unwell while they were together and disappeared in an ambulance, siren screaming, while Patrick came angry and worried back to us.

I offered to go with him to see her in hospital. And we went together on several occasions, bringing her favourite Vimto, a new colouring book, and another with the pictures coloured ready for her when it was obvious she could no longer colour them herself. Patrick was upset, nervous around her, trying to help her with going to the bathroom and angry afterwards that she was so different. He took her presents which she plucked at and didn't unwrap; he would come home and shut himself in his room. 'She had a fearsome reputation,' said a police officer later on. And she had done, she'd fought with her fists and anything she could lay her hands on, and Patrick himself had been hurt at times, though it shamed him deeply to admit it. Rachel and I were nearly the same age and we'd always got on, and one day she called me and asked me to visit her soon. She had never done such a thing before. 'Shall I come on my own this time, instead of with Patrick, so we can talk?' She was mumbling and I was afraid she had already forgotten what she'd asked. But, 'That would be nice,' she said.

Patrick had hurt Rachel badly, the hurled plate was the least of it. He had punched her in the face and broken her nose and she had taken him to court. He had been sent to prison for the offence and came out with a determination not to drink and a love for her made fiercer as well as gentler by wanting to make up for what he had done. But for all that, she was still the Rachel he thought he knew, and his relationship with her something he thought he knew, until that last stay in hospital. Love can love and yet refuse the cost and think first of itself. Rachel was a cancer patient, a vulnerable woman who needed a home, to us. But 'the Lord turned and looked at Peter' before he understood, and perhaps Patrick never understood how fragile Rachel was, until he heard the ambulance siren that morning and saw her gazing at him yellow-eyed and uncertain from a hospital bed.

✦

5

THE PILLAR

Stephen's slow and painful legs had not prevented him from getting into considerable trouble in the town, and some weeks into his stay with us he was due to appear at the local magistrates' court. Like a lot of our guests his interaction with the criminal justice system was confusing at best, and the house diary in any given week had everyone's probation appointments written in with underlinings and circles and notes to the staff on duty, particularly if it was a morning appointment and we might all have to work together to make sure they were out of bed and on their way to the probation office. Whenever one of them received a letter to say they had breached their conditions by not attending an appointment I always felt it should have been a reproach to us. And it was a help when we knew the officer, as we did Stephen's; even more so if the officer knew our guest well, and was taking an interest in their time with us, and wanting things to be different. But the system itself was beyond the understanding of all of us sometimes, and more than once I'd been to court with someone who hadn't been sure why they were there. They'd sat in the waiting area, catching up on the news with friends or avoiding eye contact with the inevitable scattering of ex-partners and exes' new partners, wanting to go out for a fag or a drink, as the day's business ticked slowly through; and I'd thought it seemed a bit unreasonable really to expect a person to be sorry when they weren't very sure what they'd done.

Going to court with Stephen was different. I'd been diffident when I offered, sensing that this proud and independent man might not want the comforting presence of a support worker as other guests had done, he was, after all, older than me, had raised two children, lost his wife nearly fifteen years ago, and been homeless almost ever since. My own life experience seemed paltry by comparison and I felt poorly equipped to be of help. It is a hard thing to accept the offer of another person to come and watch you be humiliated. Stephen not only accepted the offer, he begged me to come along.

So we went, and we sat. It was early still and the usual social scene had not arrived; eventually the duty solicitor came and chatted, and I was struck by how much of the real work is done in these conversations, before the magistrate is involved. Gently, unequivocally, he told Stephen off, 'You spat at the police officer. That really wasn't very nice, was it.' And because he was Stephen's advocate, having secured his agreement that this was so, he began to look for reasons to excuse him.

The site where the pillar is believed to have been is in a courtyard off the street at the start of the Via Dolorosa, a quiet space with trees and a church at either side, where the Roman occupation had their headquarters and soldiers came in and out of the Lions' Gate, though the name has come from the Ottomans fifteen hundred years later and the soldiers and the Jewish people would have called it something else. It isn't far from Gethsemane, and I took a short cut past it one morning going to an early Mass, but it is rather further from the place where the cock crowed, and Jesus had been up all night and would have arrived exhausted. They led Jesus there, and Pilate spoke with him and heard the crowd, and had him bound, perhaps with the same cords, to a stump of a pillar. The church over the place is known as the Church of the Condemnation, and somewhere below it you can go down and see a pavement, and think of the one which St John tells us was called in Hebrew *Gabbatha,* though the original is probably underneath.

Jesus was led to the pillar. And there are no pillars on earth he does not know, no cruelty of the world's judgements he does not perfectly comprehend; he walks with the deserving and un-deserving and their sentence is his also. He was led to the pillar, knowing what was to come; he walks with us, when the world condemns us. And he walks with us too when we come to his own judgement, with the things we have done or not done, our excuses, our feeble shame, and our fear.

There is only one pillar in the judgement of God, a pillar of mercy; and only one court of justice, a court of love. And per-haps to help us understand this, the pillar itself or one very like it is now in the chapel of the Resurrection, in the church of the Holy Sepulchre, separated by three days and the agony of the Cross from the place we are now, with Jesus bound in the court-yard just inside the city gate. We don't need much theology of atonement to see that the pillar of mercy is such because of what has been suffered between this place, and there. But full of self-hood and excuses and shame as we are, it is not easy to realize that there is no deserving or undeserving to him, no argument to be prepared in defence. Our advocate is simply our guilty plea, and the only judgement is forgiveness.

I sat in the public gallery, where Stephen could see me, and stood for the magistrates and sat again while he remained stand-ing in the dock. After that first night on the doorstep with Jacob he had always been so self-assured, cocky even, running his own life in his own way, grateful for our help but taking his own time about using it. Even waiting for a solicitor that morning he hadn't quite let go, the officer had been unreasonable, the spit had landed on his sleeve not in his eye, if he hadn't grabbed Stephen it wouldn't have happened. I'd sat with him in silence after the meeting, wondering what would happen, embarrassed for him that he'd been told off in front of me. But the Stephen in the dock was someone else, and it came to me how I might have felt if I had been there, and I found I was ashamed.

Stephen's head was down, he was respectful, 'No sir, thank you sir,' in a way I instinctively baulk at for myself, looking for a way around authority, rejecting being told what to do. In some ways I would not have been doing the work I was if I hadn't had something of this in me, because helping the undeserving poor makes people angry, and they tell you how to do it or not do it; but it is not always easy to know when we are being persecuted for righteousness' sake, and when we are allowing our own arrogance to lead us another way. And I watched Stephen and was painfully aware I could not do what he was doing, not in court if I had been there, nor with any other person in authority, and perhaps not even with God.

And I wonder how Jesus feels, when we come to him for judgement, knowing we have done wrong but wanting to keep our end up, wanting to be forgiven, but on our terms. Or when we examine our conscience, and we find some things, and other things, but what is really wanted from us is something much simpler and more difficult, our complete surrender to mercy on his terms, not ours. Perhaps we might think of the pillar, and how completely he had to surrender when he was led to it, and what that felt like; and of how it has been moved to the place of resurrection, so that we do not need to be afraid. It always seems to encourage leniency when a support worker comes to court—perhaps for the simple reason that the defendant seems to belong somewhere and it's easier to send them home than anywhere else—and Stephen and I left the court together soon after, and it was nearly time for lunch. 'Well done,' I said, hoping I wasn't being patronizing, that this was what he wanted to hear. Stephen had no such doubts. 'Thank you so much for coming with me,' he said.

6

THE SCOURGE

Milee cut herself badly a couple of weeks after she came to stay, with a razor blade and a bit of broken glass, slashes across her thighs under her pyjamas. The flesh had been parted well below the skin and it took more effort than I usually needed to look from there to the first-aid box, find some suitable bandages, calmly patching her up as I might have done if she'd fallen in the street and come home with a graze. She refused A&E before I'd finished suggesting it, already distancing herself from the wounds she'd inflicted. 'Can't you sort of squidge them together or something,' barely flinching as I cleaned them with alcohol wipes, a sting which had brought Stephen to tears. We talk a lot in this kind of work about lived experience, and triggers, but that can be a simplification; each of us processes the past differently at different times, and for me, I have found that when it comes to it the need in front of me is all that really matters. The immediate question seemed to be why Milee had been cutting that particular evening, when I could see she had done the same thing many other times before.

We sat on the sofa. 'What happened today?' I asked, not really expecting an answer. But she seemed to want to talk. She'd seen her uncle in town, he'd asked if she was still on the game, she said it was £20. He said he'd give her £10, so she'd agreed to a BJ only, and they'd gone into the toilets at the multistorey car park, and he'd taken over and penetrated her. 'Has he done this before?' I asked, thinking of hours of sanitized safeguarding training, of how we're not to investigate, but pass on disclosures, and what to do if the survivor is at immediate risk of harm. The harm seemed to have happened already. And she talked, caught between detachment and seeming to need me to understand, about her uncle, her mother's brother, who had started her working. 'How old were you?' She was eleven, and she'd lost her first child, his child, when she was twelve, a tiny foetus in the woods by the dark path along the old railway line, walking home from school. 'I just buried it in the leaves.' There are times when nothing we can say seems at all helpful and in the silence we almost sense the angels come into the room, and kneel, and weep.

The scourge, unlike the pillar to which Jesus was bound to receive it, has not survived for pilgrims to see among the precious relics collected at the time or gathered since. It has taken its place instead in the second of the sorrowful mysteries of the rosary, a scene almost indecent to look at in twenty-first-century Britain, unlike in Spain or southern Italy where artists have painted or sculpted for their churches as realistic an image as possible, a shocking reminder that the reality would have been both brutal and indecent and very much worse than we let ourselves imagine. And yet it is essential that we do try to imagine, and more than that, to begin to understand this scene in the light not only of that spring morning in Jerusalem but of God's great love.

Jesus was scourged with thirty-nine lashes, a punishment which must have seemed to him, and perhaps even to some of those present, to go on, and on, and on. And when we say that Jesus suffered for us, it is worth our thinking of this, because what we are saying is that, blow by blow, this is what we have deserved, and which happened to him instead. We are missing the point of penance if we try to punish ourselves for the things for which we feel guilty. Jesus has done all our penance already, and the little inconveniences we take on are only to help us understand that; because what he wants from us is a sorrow for our sins which comes only from understanding better what he has done.

Yet we can ask God to chasten us, because in our self-will we do not yet see our sins as he does, and as we begin to follow Jesus more closely we realize that we need his help. We ask, but we are not asking God to make bad things happen to us, or for some endorsement of our self-loathing and guilt. No—what we are asking for is the chastening which comes with understanding better what Jesus has suffered, with our growing realization of how much our self-regard and determined self-will have pained his unconditional love. We are asking to see ourselves as Jesus sees us, and this will hurt us far more, as we grow to love him, than anything we might suffer if we did not. We begin to see what his love for us really means. The chastisement our God gives us when we ask is nothing less than the transformational awakening of grace.

✦

Milee was expecting her seventh child. The baby stillborn or mis-carried on that dark evening after school had been the first, and the sixth had been lost at four months' term in the toilet at the home she'd left. Two had lived, and been loved, and been taken into care; she kept their photos and remembered their birthdays and grieved for her loss. And the others had also been lost pre-maturely, tiny lives slipping from a body too young, or too exhausted, to bear them. She told her story dry-eyed that even-ing, matter-of-fact, one thing, and then another. I might have been deceived if I had not seen the cuts on her legs. 'It's not your fault,' I said at last. She said nothing, but later I found a note folded small on the floor outside my office. 'I feel so dirty,' it said.

Milee was not unusual with her razor and broken glass; we used a lot of first-aid supplies looking after our guests and I reflected sometimes that the wounds which anger inflicts on others are no less grievous when turned inward on oneself. Trauma, so much a part of the past for the people we cared for, can create a terrible anger, and so perpetuate itself in a chain which it seems sometimes only a miracle can stop. We might look on in pity, and think, how tragic, thank goodness that's not me. But the truth is that none of us walks through this world unwounded and unwounding, and none of us is without need of help.

To walk from Gethsemane to the place of the scourging we must pass the pools of Bethesda, the 'house of mercy' with its porticoes, where Jesus met the man who had lain there for thirty-eight years. And he said to the man, 'Do you want to be healed?' and the man started to talk about his past and present problems, he couldn't get to the pool, people pushed in first, and goodness knows what else. Jesus interrupted with a simple 'Take up your mat and walk.' Perhaps the point of the Gospel story is that we take our sickness of heart sometimes to the wrong places, and forget that what we need is already with us in the presence of God. A year later Milee had been crying on the telephone and talking about how she had hurt herself, with a broken plate, a tin can, a rubber hose. I said what I hoped were the right professional things about trying to connect her with counselling, and talking to her midwife, but after a time, weary and wanting the conversation to end, I interrupted with what seemed to me to be the most banal of reassurances, 'It will pass some time, you know. You won't always feel this way.' But later came a text which I would never have believed she could write: 'You opened a door for me today.'

✦

7

THE CROWN OF THORNS

It was four years since I'd first met Marta, on a dark winter's night in the year before the pandemic when, like most similar places in the country, we had opened in the evening only, dormitory beds for the night with a cold expulsion every morning. She was somewhat drunk and had very little English, and as my Lithuanian and Russian were so poor as to be unable to distinguish between the two, we were making slow progress. After a time she pulled down her tracksuit trousers at the front desk where I was sitting, and pointing vigorously to the problem she repeated firmly, 'Police!' I looked at the deep black bruises which covered her behind and started a call on 101 while we made her a cup of tea. The police sent two male officers whom I steered into a side room, and who with increasing impatience tried to make sense of her story; they left when Marta, sobbing and unable to articulate the English words she knew, backed against a wall and refused to say any more.

It was only really in the last year that we'd come to know something of her story. She came from a Russian family, brought up in care in Lithuania in some kind of children's home; her brother, or foster brother, had also stayed with us and came back one evening with a stab wound. She'd been expecting a baby, once, in Lithuania; she'd been beaten up, and lost the child. She'd come to England to work and had been in and out of agency jobs on the Fenland farms during the time we'd known her, ten- or twelve-hour days, bringing us sometimes a bag of lumpy carrots, or a sheaf of overgrown leeks. I used to see the 'Locally Grown' signs in the vegetable section of the local supermarket, decorated with the Union Jack, and think of Marta's raw red hands, and wince. Her alcoholism grew gradually worse and her collapses more frequent; the last time we'd closed for the summer she hadn't understood, and come home anyway, and shortly after with an ambulance on its way I'd done CPR for the first time, with Marta lying half on the gravel, half on the grass.

And yet how she could joke. She made the language barrier into a game; understanding more English than she spoke, she used it to tease us. She pretended to pinch things from the staff desk, the diary, notes; once, my laptop, and I lost my sense of humour, and she cried. She chatted up the male staff, who were used to her, and the male volunteers, who were sometimes a little taken aback: she was indiscriminate, a former headmaster, a magistrate, and when she began to spend more time in hospital, the male nurses and doctors. And she was kind, and perceptive: the day when Milee felt the new baby move inside her, and was afraid she might lose this one also, and curled on the sofa speaking to no-one, Marta tried to ask her what was wrong. She drew tears on her face with her finger, to show she understood. Then she rumpled up her yellow hair, took two lemons from the kitchen, and holding them on her chest she stuck out her front and swung her hips and said in what she must have thought was a sexy voice, 'Pamela Anderson!' I looked at Milee, and saw her mouth twitch, and suddenly we were all three laughing.

✦

The church which remembers the crowning with thorns is on the same site as the Church of the Flagellation, at the start of the Via Dolorosa, off the street and with a courtyard between. It is a quiet, shady place; under the cypresses I saw a bishop resting on a hot day, a moment apart from the hard labour of shepherding other pilgrims. The church itself is small, and domed; inside, the dome is covered in a mosaic of gold, with the crown of thorns encircling it, and from the thorns blood is dripping, and above this the thorns have filled the dome with white blossom. I thought of it the next spring in England, when mid-way through Lent the blackthorn hedges frothed over with white flowers.

The crown of thorns itself is now in the Cathédrale de Notre Dame, in Paris; perhaps it was our Lady who carried it away from the place of crucifixion, when the body was laid in her arms and made hastily ready for the tomb. The thorns have long since been broken off as relics, the crown itself is a bare circle of twigs. And yet there is a crown for all of us, if we will wear it, and thorns as precious, if we see them for what they are.

We are all called to be saints. 'Be perfect as your heavenly Father is perfect', and, probably far more than we realize, we read into this our own ideals of perfection, mostly about trying harder, and being the best we can be for someone else to approve. We forget that God has made us perfect to begin with, as part of his perfect creation; the problem is not that we need to become something else, but that our self-will and sin and our own foolish ideas are spoiling what he has made. We are looking for crowns, and Jesus shows us what the most precious of all crowns looks like. We look for jewels, and Jesus shows us thorns, and his own face, bleeding.

✦

I worked very hard with both Marta and Milee. I went with them to doctor's appointments, midwife appointments, hospital appointments; I talked to debt collectors, immigration support workers, social workers, substance misuse workers, tenancy support workers, and the police. In any usual sense I went above and beyond for them both, and at some cost, as the local authority never accepted that Milee had nowhere safe to stay, even when a police detective backed her case and her housing association were obliged to agree to a tenancy transfer.

I came in for a lot of criticism from council officers, usually at second hand where I could offer no defence. In the end she stayed with us until after the baby was born, and she had recovered from the birth to manage the move; which meant I had the privilege of taking her to hospital, and coming back in the afternoon to see how she was, and how the baby was, after the C-section. I found her smoking in the bus stop opposite and thought we must have got the day wrong, until she showed me her bed, and the cot, upstairs. The little girl was sleeping, and tiny, and perfect.

The church at Bethlehem is one of the oldest in the world, built in the last days of the Roman empire, massive without, rich with mosaics and hanging lamps within. Its door is famously so tiny that only children can enter without stooping; 'unless you become like little children you shall not enter the kingdom of heaven'. There is no space to take our pride with us when we come to worship the Christ child, no room for the false crowns of our sophisticated world. We must take them off. And then to go to the place of the Nativity we must go downstairs, into a cave; the place is on the floor, the cave is low, we must kneel on the ground, where there is a jewelled and shining silver star.

There are stars in the dome of the crown of thorns too, in that place not of birth but of going to die. Pinpoint windows in the ceiling, tiny, bright with daylight, in among the blossoming thorns. We might call to mind there our efforts in this world, of how we try to be the best, sometimes with such very good intentions. We might even thank God for the good which has come from our work. But until we realize that all these good things we bring to the manger are only what God has first given us, we will not understand the love of God for what it really is. We sometimes talk of humility as something to be afraid of, something very painful, and solemn, and hard won. And so it is, but it is also the self-forgetfulness of a homeless migrant worker in temporary accommodation making a frightened mother smile with two lemons and no concern if she was laughed at or not. It is the glimpse of joy we sometimes have, when we realize that the crown is bursting into flower, and full of stars, and that to enter the kingdom of heaven all that is asked of us is to leave all our baggage outside and enter the little door with perfect child-like trust.

+

8

THE WASHED HANDS

I usually covered the Friday morning shift at work, but there were two days of the year I made especially sure of on the staff rota, partly to give the rest of the team a break on a public holiday, and partly as a reminder to myself of why we were doing the work we did. One of these days was Christmas Day, and the other was Good Friday. Christmas was often a difficult day for our residents, the town silent, the day full of painful memories. Good Friday on the other hand seemed always to be bright, and full of spring sunshine; the town was busy with the first day of the long weekend, and quite often seemed to coincide with people's benefit payments so that there was money to spend and alcohol in the streets and comings and goings at our door. The first Good Friday, Jerusalem on the eve of the Passover filled with visitors in holiday mood, must have felt quite similar.

Philippa arrived on our doorstep half-way through the morning. I had known her as long as I'd been in the job, she had stayed with us most winters, a few nights, then absent, until we felt we couldn't keep her room empty any longer and gave it to someone else. She went to prison sometimes for shoplifting when the court ran out of other options; she came out, and carried on, because addiction is a pitiless expense. Her probation officer had called us the day before, asking us to look out for her; she was staying with a former partner, and the officer suspected that violence was involved, and that she might be paying with favours for a roof over her head. She stood on the doorstep, emaciated, dirty, in a

30

broken pair of flip flops. The sun was shining but she was shivering. She smiled brightly and asked if there was any chance of a coffee.

I fetched the coffee, and some food. I called the council's out-of-hours housing team while she ate, and was grateful to be busy with something rather than try to chat while she was eating. The food disappeared in seconds, and I fetched some more, embarrassed that she'd had to ask. I described her situation and, walking away a little so she couldn't hear, I described what she looked like. And I met the wall which she had expected, and had told me would happen, but which I had insisted we should try to argue with; no, she hadn't been rough sleeping, or at any rate had no proof, she'd had help many times before, and there was to be no more. And I was ashamed: for ourselves, who had no spare room; for the provision for the homeless in that town which we were a part of, and which could or would not provide for her; for our society, which washed its hands of some of the people who needed help the most. She smiled even more brightly, 'Oh well, don't worry.' Then she asked me if we had a spare coat.

✦

Pilate is an unsettling character. At first glance he seems so far removed from us, a pagan governor in a toga, worshipping gods whose names now are the ruined temples of antiquity, part of an empire confined to history one-and-a-half thousand years since. And yet. He asks questions. His wife has a strange dream, and tells him. He comes under great pressure from the crowd. He tries to bargain and fails, and he tries to absolve himself of his own decision. 'You would have no power over me had it not been given you from above,' says Jesus to him, and no wonder Pilate 'sought to release him'. We are not told what was going through the heads of the soldiers that day, or the disciples. But we are told what Pilate thought, and his behaviour is disconcertingly familiar.

The Antonia fortress, where the judgement is thought to have been made, is across the street from the Church of the Condemnation: every Friday, the Franciscan priests gather in the playground of the primary school now on the site, and begin the Stations of the Cross. The neighbourhood is Arab, and crumbling, and poor. Grandmothers sell green figs in baskets, sitting on the street. But the only street fountain we found in the Old City is also there, with a sign helpfully translated: 'this is the water fountain of the prophet Muhammad.' We splashed our hot faces. Pilate, nearby, once called for water to wash his hands.

Jesus, questioned by Pilate, fell silent. And in this silence is much more than a refusal to argue with a ruler who wasn't worth very much, because what we must understand is that it was our sins of which he stood accused in that place, not his own, whatever the people who brought him there might have intended. Jesus is silent because he is going to Calvary for us, and there is nothing to be said in our defence. When we come to prepare for confession we might think of him there before Pilate, and of his silence, the space for our own list of sins. Jesus is silent, and even as Pilate washed his hands of him, his own hands were grasping the Cross.

I found an old coat which Philippa said she liked, but she needed shoes. We set off into town together, she shuffling patiently beside me, and I making conversation probably more cheerfully than was natural, because it was Good Friday, and I was fasting, and conscious that I had a headache, and that unlike Philippa I was fasting by choice. We reached the bus station, and then we ran into a problem. Philippa wasn't allowed in shoe shops, she said. She was banned from all shops in town, because of the shoplifting.

We devised a solution. The first shop was awkward, the shoes couldn't be seen from the street. I bought her some, and she tried them on sitting on a bench outside, and they were no good, so I went back in for a refund. The second shop was better, plate glass, cheap trainers near the door. I went in and held up various pairs. She signed to me through the window, thumbs up, and I paid and took them out to her. She put them on at once, and we left the flip flops, and the box, in a nearby bin. And she left me there, 'Thank you so much for your help.' We had no empty room, and she knew very well when she'd had all the help I was likely to give. I started walking back through the bank holiday crowds, feeling pleased with myself, and then I heard singing. The local churches' walk of witness was coming slowly up the high street, carrying a large wooden cross.

And it is so often when we wash our hands, when we abandon responsibility and further effort and cease to look for the right thing to do next, that we find ourselves grasped by God. We cannot look at that scene with Pilate, of silent response and turning to the Cross, without seeing something of the immense love which held us that day even as Jesus stood exhausted, bleeding from the scourging, and yet with one purpose to fulfil. Our God does not abandon us. 'What is truth?' asked Pilate, but the truth was that it was there in front of him. We cannot wash our hands of the love of God for us. I thought of Philippa, and I looked at the procession on the high street. And I saw that among the singing crowd were people who were homeless and staying with us.

✦

9

THE CROSS

Milee smoked crack cocaine most days. She kept a crack pipe in the staff cupboard, and asked for it when she needed it to take out with her; not a perfect solution, but the best way we had of trying to make sure she wasn't bringing drugs into the house, and of trying to involve her in that aim. On a good day she would go out once or twice, sometimes no further than an abandoned car park across the street. On a bad day she would be in and out all day and most of the night, and grew more argumentative, more paranoid, and louder as the night wore on. She was frank about her drug use, and didn't mind questions. I was tentative. 'How much does it cost each time?' I asked, feeling I was being intrusive. 'Forty quid it should be,' she said, the price for two clients, or one if they wanted something extra. It was no good feeling embarrassed by her candour. She needed us to be there for her, where she was, and I remembered she'd been twenty years on the job.

But then she was expecting. And with no experience of my own to help I found myself in the front line of support, with midwife appointments, hospital appointments, social worker appointments. Milee refused to see them all.

We learn a lot about other people's professions when we see them tested, and I saw a lot of professionals over the next few months. Midwives who came to visit at home when Milee wouldn't go to them, patiently coming again a few days later because from her safe place on the house sofa she had refused to lift her clothes. A social worker who said not to worry when Milee had been rude and racist in an unexpected home visit and I'd called afterwards to apologize, 'Don't worry, I will refer her to my colleague, the important thing is she has someone she's ok with.' Safeguarding advisors from the county council, who organized panel meetings, which took hours to consider what Milee and I both knew was the inevitable outcome once the baby was born. And a specialist social worker, deceptively laid back, who at last persuaded Milee to talk about the baby and what was happening next.

✦

The Via Dolorosa which begins at the Church of the Condemnation is narrow, and steeply uphill. The souks, something like an indoor market, cluster each side; much of it is roofed overhead. Spices, incense, olive wood carvings, are piled in the street, shopkeepers call out, pilgrims trek after their leaders, young men rush up and down on scooters piled implausibly high with crates, veiled women walk with bowed heads taking shopping home. There are faces everywhere, inches from one's own. You cannot see very far ahead, and you have to watch your feet, and your pockets. There is nothing otherworldly about the road where Jesus carried the Cross. He dragged it uphill, through the faces of the crowds, for about half a mile.

Jesus said, 'My yoke is easy and my burden is light.' And this extraordinary statement makes sense only when we realize that this terrible burden was carried for the one reason that he chose it for himself, and chose it for love. Most of us know that doing some small inconvenient service is not tiresome when we do it for someone we love; we stay up late to finish or wrap a present, we give up time to help when we're needed, we go without something we wanted to give them a gift we know they will like. Of all the things our guests lacked, having nobody to give things to seemed sometimes to be what they missed the most.

35

We can look at Jesus carrying the Cross, and we can understand in part. But yet we wonder what good this suffering can be to us. And Jesus says, 'Whoever does not carry the cross and follow me cannot be my disciple.'

Love does not allow us to carry our cross alone. Jesus carried all our crosses that day, but more than that, he carries them with us now. Taking up our own cross is our response to this love, and our acceptance that coming after Jesus means coming with him to Calvary, but also beyond, to where his love will bring us. Sometimes our cross seems obvious to us, a grief to be endured, an illness or loss to be accepted. But sometimes this is not so, and it might take someone else to point out that something we have struggled with terribly is also a chance to walk with God. We must ask for help to recognize our cross, because if we do, we have his promise that everything will be different.

✦

The hospital appointment, the first scan, was the hardest thing. Milee had refused to go, every time I tried to encourage her: the date was wrong, she didn't get on with the midwife on duty, she didn't have money for the machine which prints photos. We went anyway, and perhaps my ignorance of the whole procedure helped her, because she had to show me where to go, and explain the process, and when I squeaked in surprise as the baby's picture appeared on the screen she squirmed with laughter so much the midwife had to put the gel on her stomach all over again. And the photo, in a yellow card with an elephant on the front and a bow, turned out to be free of charge. I said I thought the elephant was an exaggeration, at four months. And she laughed again all the way home.

I suppose I thought, before Milee came to stay, that pregnant women who were homeless would be accommodated by their local authority in some suitable place for bringing up the baby. And perhaps this is the case, if children's services believe the mother can care for the child. But a homeless mother cannot care for a child, and having no address becomes one reason among many why she may not be allowed to: before the litany of sadness which alcohol, drugs and the risks of how she obtains them are added to the picture. I fought a battle with her housing association for Milee to be offered a tenancy transfer after she said she could not go home; and we won it, though after the panel meetings and only just before the baby was due. Children's services followed their own schedule and simply planned a home for the child.

And I think she knew all along that this was how it would be. She loved the baby, had named her long before that first scan, and the crack cocaine and the risks she took to obtain it were not so much a rejection of responsibility as a part of how she coped with living which she could not cope without. She spent only one night in hospital after the C-section, and she spent part of that out the back, smoking crack which one of her clients had brought her. She put the baby on her breast that night, and the next day the baby was taken into intensive care in drug withdrawal. Milee phoned us. She wanted to die, she said, she would jump off the hospital roof, she couldn't stay there. I knew nothing about recovery time from C-sections, or what she would need. I said I would be with her in twenty minutes, and took her home to us.

✦

10

THE SEAMLESS ROBE

I came to work one Saturday afternoon and found the house in a state of exasperation and concern, Stephen had been up all night, in and out all morning, arguing with anyone who spoke to him, and had kept falling asleep at the dining table until he'd finally gone up to bed. Or not exactly falling asleep; falling into the semi-conscious state we often saw when people had taken a lot of drugs, eyes half closed, head going down on the table, roused with difficulty. I went upstairs to check that he was ok.

He was sitting on the edge of his bed, just. He turned his head when I came in and muttered something, and I caught him by one shoulder as he fell. He lolled against me, heavier than he looked, no longer responding when I said his name. I wriggled my phone from my pocket and called an ambulance. And I saw the note lying open on his pillow, addressed to the girlfriend he sometimes went to for comfort and for drugs, beginning clearly and straggling into oblivion at the end. Stephen had taken his bank holiday weekend medication in one go—the last time he'd overdosed, I'd persuaded him to change to a daily pick-up script, but they always gave him Friday's tablets with Saturday and Sunday in the packet too—and he was grieving terribly, and felt he could not go on. He was far more candid on paper than he was in conversation, the writing was raw. He was still leaning on my arm, and I ached as I tried to stop him falling on the floor.

The ambulance came quickly, as remarkably they always seemed to when we needed them most. Stephen, who said he

38

hated hospitals, and had been too scared to go that night we took off his bandages on the front doorstep, was strapped into a chair, and somehow lifted down the stairs. I suggested I could go too, and the paramedics closed with the offer at once, glad to be able to complete the forms about date of birth, medical history and so on more efficiently in the back of the ambulance as the blue lights rushed us up the road. I'd never been driven on blue lights before. The driver chatted casually through to his colleague in the back as we swung through gaps in the traffic and Stephen lay oblivious to it all, unconscious on the stretcher.

And so we emerge from the steep narrow street, and come into a courtyard bright with white stone and the growing heat of the day, and into the Church of the Holy Sepulchre. The site was originally an old rock quarry by a graveyard, outside the city wall; preserved in memory by the Roman emperor Hadrian with a temple of Venus — an ironic choice for a place which knew such love — and later covered with a church by Constantine, and then by the Crusaders after the first church had been destroyed. It contains the places both of the Crucifixion and the Resurrection, under one roof and with very little distance between the two. Jesus on the other hand would have seen rough ground, and rocks, and the city of Jerusalem downhill and to the east behind him, where the sun which had risen over the Mount of Olives and Gethsemane was now high in the sky. And there the soldiers pulled off all his clothes.

The seamless robe which Jesus wore, and its stripping from his exhausted body, has meant a great deal since; venerated both in France and in Russia, it is treasured as a reminder of the indivisible nature of Christ, and his stripping as a sign of the self-emptying love which went to Calvary for us. But for the crowd on that Friday morning, the uncovering of his body showed very clearly something else: the bruises, the blood, the wounds from the lashes on his back laid bare. They would have looked, and seen at once how terribly he had been hurt.

And we might think of what they saw, in the times when we have done something wrong and realize we don't really feel sorry; or when we hide from ourselves what we have done wrong, because we don't like to see it. We might think of this scene, and ask for the grace to see how our sins have hurt Jesus, not because it matters very much what our feelings are, but because this grace will help us also in the lifelong process of being stripped of our pretensions with God. We ask, and we look at him. And our asking is in itself a beginning, of setting aside feelings and prevarications and seeing that what is asked of us is our complete honesty, our real self with all our wounds. We see, and we begin to understand that this is what God sees, just as we see him. And we cannot bear to give him anything else.

✦

Stephen had a complicated relationship with the local hospital, as well as being afraid of it. Some weeks earlier I had succeeded in taking him to A&E after an abscess in his groin had burst; his jeans were soaked with the result and he was in terrible pain. We went through triage and the evening was getting on and I made the mistake of leaving him, thinking that having come this far he would wait more or less patiently for his turn. An hour later he began to panic and thought he'd had to wait so long because nobody realized he needed help, so he went back to reception and pulled down his trousers to show the problem, as he'd done for us, wanting someone to see that it hurt. The receptionist called hospital security and he was bundled out into the road. I tried, that week, to persuade them he hadn't meant to be offensive. I hit a wall of official letters. Stephen was banned from the hospital, only to be permitted 'life and limb' care.

And there we were, very much in life and limb care, in the resuscitation bay at A&E reserved only for people who needed most immediate help. I glanced around as Stephen was wheeled in. There were three other beds, all occupied by young men. The single nurse set us up quickly, and left; curtains were pulled, and one of the men began to scream in pain. Stephen and I were alone. I watched his breathing, and noticed a panic button I could press, if it stopped. After some time a junior doctor came in, looking harassed. 'I'm Stephen's support worker,' I said, 'please tell me if I can do anything useful to help. He has an ab-scess in his groin which might be infected and he's taken three days' worth of his prescription drugs and probably some others too.' The doctor glanced at his notes. 'Could you take his trousers off please, the nurse is busy? And his top?' I hesitated. Stephen would be embarrassed if he knew, or worse. I put on some gloves. The jeans were tight around the bandages on his calves. I tugged harder, they were good jeans, he would not want them cut. The doctor was in a hurry, needing to take bloods. 'Can you hold this arm down please, I need to find a vein.' I hated needles, and I knew that if Stephen was injecting in his groin, it was because he could no longer do so easily in his arm. I gripped his hand hard against the bed.

✦

11

THE DICE

Milee was offered a new tenancy in March, and although it was to be another two months before it was ready for her, she was asked to go and see it before she could confirm that she accepted it. It seemed an easy task to me, used to renting properties, and knowing what to look for on a viewing; but she had never done such a thing before, having always lived in whatever place she was told. It was in a village outside town, which she said herself she thought would keep her safer, and on a bus route to the hospital, which was a relief to me. I took her in the car that first time, the sun shone, and she looked at the hazy green in the fields, the blossom on the hedgerows, and started to talk about a children's home in Wales where she'd learned to ride, she loved animals. We looked at the house together, with me asking the questions, 'Will the kitchen be repaired? where is the oil tank?' Milee seemed overwhelmed. 'We'll give her a voucher so she can decorate,' said the lady from the housing association, looking sympathetic. I glanced at the baby bump and felt doubtful. Milee was looking out of the window at the field behind the house, and the horses.

She came back into the present very suddenly on the way home, looking at a message on her phone. 'Barry says there's a load of police cars outside the house and paramedics and stuff and everyone's there watching.' 'Oh dear,' I said, pulling up at the traffic lights, 'is Barry normally reliable?' Barry was one of her clients. I thought of the two staff I'd left on duty, neither as confident as they might be, with a load of police cars and all the rest. I left the car in the church car park next door and ran to the scene.

Jamie was lying there in the garden, a man we knew a little, mainly as the friend of others who had stayed with us. He was with Stephen, and both the staff, and the first responders on their motorbike, and an ambulance, and the police. The garden fence was crowded with people we knew, and teenagers we knew by sight, looking on. And he was lying on his back, and his face was grey, and the first responders and the ambulance crew were trying to get him breathing while a police inspector stood by, his colleagues respectfully behind. Stephen came to tell me what had happened at once, 'He's had a heart attack Luce, I did the kiss of life.' My colleague followed him and added her own story, 'I tried to do chest compressions and Stephen was drunk and kept getting in the way.' I cleared the crowd from the fence, told the other staff to go and rest inside for a moment, reassured Stephen, spoke with the police. Jamie breathed with the machine but didn't regain consciousness. They put him in the ambulance, and drove away.

On the pavement in the Church of the Condemnation we can see the scratchings of a board game, a game with dice, made by Roman soldiers with time to kill, or a gamble to win. The banality of the markings surprises us, and their closeness; a soldier's hand reached out just here to carve the lines, a soldier's feet crouched just there to play. Perhaps the soldiers on Calvary scratched something similar in the rock to pass the time while the three bodies hung above them, or perhaps they just rolled the dice for the seamless robe, and then put games away. We think of the things they carried with them, as Jesus carried the Cross: a hammer, some nails, and dice, in case they were bored. We can so easily grow accustomed to the suffering of others, and the suffering we cause.

The soldiers crouched on the ground in the place they had brought Jesus to die, and they rolled dice to see which of them would keep his clothes. We look on in horror, and yet if we are to be honest with ourselves, we will see we are no different. We gamble with so many precious things in our lives, our time, other people's generosity and patience, our place in heaven, our souls; we gamble that we won't be found out, or face consequences. And we play these games while others suffer, and we look the other way, intent on our own agenda. We have a God to crucify. And we ask which of us will win and keep his clothes.

✦

Jamie never regained consciousness in hospital, he had stopped breathing for too long and the first responders who had taken over from the attempts of Stephen and my colleague had come too late. They turned off his oxygen in intensive care and let him fade into the night. It was hard, watching the CCTV of the scene in the garden and writing my report for the inquest, hard not to be angry with the staff who had tried to help him when he came for a sandwich and collapsed at our door. I wished I had been there. I wasn't, and if I had been, very likely I would have managed no better. I knew Jamie only a little from his visits to our door, I was sorry he was gone. I was much sorrier that I hadn't helped, and I didn't want to go to the funeral.

But Frank did, the young man caught in county lines, who I'd sent away after he sold crack to Milee. He hadn't spoken to me since, angry that I'd chosen her over himself, but I saw him in the street one evening, and he was crying for Jamie. I spoke with him, and he was wary. I didn't like it when our guests thought I'd been unfair, my pride was hurt, I wanted to do something to be in the right again. The funeral was in a couple of days' time, and I offered him a lift.

Then Milee had an unexpected appointment with the midwives. I took her there, and I messaged Frank to say where I was, and that I'd be back in time to collect him. The hospital took longer than expected. I was late coming back, and the other staff told me that Frank had been and gone. And of course I could easily have left Milee with the bus fare home, and come back for Frank. I'd decided not to. I wanted to do a good job with her, and I didn't care as much about him. I saw Frank later that day. 'You fucking said you'd take me, I don't care, I found someone else.' I'd thought Frank and Jamie were no closer than two mates in a group of chaotic people who did drugs together. I was wrong. Frank was shocked at Jamie's death, and frightened for himself. They gambled with their lives every time they bought drugs, never really knowing what was in them. I gambled every time I put my pride first, or made a promise and broke it; and we might think these things don't matter very much, but the fact is that if we go our own way once, we shall soon be tempted to do the same when the stakes are higher, and we will yield to the temptation. We were all three dicing with death. And luck can run out.

✦

12

THE TITLE

It was winter, and Simon was camping in a wood. He came to us one evening, well organized, a flask for us to fill with boiling water so he could make a drink in the night, layers of clothing, all his possessions packed into one tattered rucksack. He had been one of our volunteers, and had been staying with his brother, who asked him to leave when the police came to arrest him. We hadn't seen him for two years. We took him in as soon as we had a vacancy, knowing he had no chance of accommodation anywhere else. He was an easy guest, appreciating everything, keen to help with anything he could. He was cheerful, upbeat, had joined a church study group, followed with alacrity the latest troubles of the local football team. The weeks went by, and we waited for the court date. And sometimes in the night, he let us see how much he was scared.

The summons when it came was for the city Crown Court, the morning session. It meant a very early bus and I arranged to meet him there, 9 a.m. in the car park outside. He was in the smartest things he had, a carrier bag in his hand with his medication and a water bottle. He had left everything else in the house with us. It was a cold February morning but he was damp with sweat, and trembling. I knew there was nothing I would be able to do to lessen whatever sentence the judge would impose: no mitigating circumstances I could offer, no hope that the simple presence of a support worker would help as it had so often in the magistrates' courts when I'd gone with others and we'd left at the end together, a custodial sentence avoided, another chance given. But Simon had never been to court before, and was beyond working it all out that day, so I checked the court lists and showed him where to go, and explained how it worked and when he would be called, watching the progress of the morning's cases on a screen. And was thankful to find some-one to represent him, when I discovered that crown courts unlike magistrates' courts do not have a duty solicitor on hand on the day for people too chaotic or poor or perplexed to have organized their own. It was too quiet in the waiting area, and the café was far away on the magistrates' side of the building. I missed the companionable chaos of the court I knew.

I knew the facts of what Simon had done. But it is one thing to know the facts, an honest summary of what he had told me as part of his referral to stay with us. The purpose of that conversa-tion had been to learn what we needed to know to complete a risk assessment and to support him. The whole truth, as read by the prosecution, was intended to convict him.

I listened to the account of the trap that had been set by an on-line group of paedophile-catchers, as they called themselves. How they had posed as 14-year-old Rosie in year 9, and how Simon had started chatting with her about sex, and what it was like, and told her how to penetrate herself with her fingers. And eventually, had arranged to meet up, and was arrested at home before the date agreed. The trap was undoubtedly a grim work of people who knew what they were doing and how far to take a person to make sure the line for a prison sentence had been crossed, and I wondered at the moral rights and wrongs of bringing someone to trial for a crime against a victim who did not exist. But as the texts back and forth were read aloud, and Simon sat bowed over with his face in his hands, I felt my stomach turn sick with revul-sion. I remembered very well what it had been like to be a fourteen-year-old girl, in year nine. Simon was fifty-three.

✦

The title which was written over Jesus's head on the Cross is precious among the things from that day in being left to us, not entire, but enough to read it 'in Greek and in Latin' both lettered so poorly as to suggest the title is indeed authentic—for surely nobody would put the letters back to front, right to left as Hebrew is written, with spelling mistakes, unless they were doing their best in a hurry in foreign languages with someone telling them to get on with it. The relic is kept with a nail, and a thorn, in a chapel at the top of a flight of steps in the church of Santa Croce in Rome, the church the emperor Constantine's mother founded on her return from Jerusalem to house the treasures she had brought home. A child who lost a leg to bone cancer is buried at the entrance. And you go up the steps, past the Stations of the Cross, to reach the place.

But the extraordinary thing about the title and its script is that it contained far more of the truth than Pilate ever intended. 'What I have written, I have written,' he said: and he had written both the truth everyone knew, and that which Jesus alone knew of himself. That he was 'Jesus of Nazareth' was clear to anyone. That he was 'King of the Jews' was fully known only to himself, to God. 'What is truth?' Pilate had asked; little knowing that he was to answer his own question. And that is the title under which Jesus died: his name, and the crime he had committed. We might think of the two unknown thieves on either side of him, perhaps with their names also written over their heads, followed by their crime, 'Thief.'

And so we climb to Calvary, and the climb is our preparation for confession. Perhaps we are accustomed to write down what we have to say, to take with us as a help if we are nervous; perhaps we just make a list to help our preparations. Or perhaps we have very little to say, but know that little so well that we have no need to write it down. We climb to Calvary, and we add our sins to the script over the Cross. The things which will have been obvious to others, 'I lost my temper, I was lazy.' The things we think no-one knows but ourselves, 'I was jealous, I lied.' Here is the title which will be fixed over his head, 'Jesus of Nazareth, King of the Jews,' with all the misery we have brought to be added beneath. When we say that Jesus died for our sins, we mean no more or less than this.

✦

I went to see Simon two weeks later. The visiting process seemed to be much easier than when I went to see Patrick, the black sniffer Labradors had gone, and we were left alone in a room for nearly an hour. The window was tightly closed, and the air was stale. I asked for a glass of water, and tried to focus.

Visits to prison are so much about everyday things. Messages to people Simon knew, whom he wanted to know he was there, and others whom he didn't want to know. What he wanted done with his belongings. The latest football score—how daft I'd been not to check that. What the food was like, and his roommate, and what it was like having diarrhoea in a toilet in the corner of a small cell you have to share. The form he had to fill in, if he wanted to be able to phone us. The job he was hoping for, helping in the prison market garden, for a wage of £8 a week. I was worried he'd have grief from other prisoners for what he'd done, and expected him at least to be sharing with someone convicted for similar offences. He seemed perplexed. It didn't seem to be the done thing, to ask what other people were in prison for. It was something in the past, in a previous life, and much less interesting than the present reality he was in. It was Shrove Tuesday, and I said I'd come back in a few weeks, after Easter.

But perhaps there was already something of Easter in that close little room, where Simon was describing the people he'd met, and where for the first time what they'd done had no relevance except that it had brought them here. I had come away from court sad, and troubled by what I'd heard; I left the prison

49

feeling I had met something else, and was unsurprised when the sun came out from a week of rain clouds as I was leaving and poured over the city below. Dwelling on the sins of others can leave us angry and depressed. When we recall our own, and write the whole truth we know of them over the head of Jesus on the Cross, they become not only a part of our salvation, but our precious gifts to him. The present, and the future, are what matter now. His perfect generosity challenges our own, and Jesus on the Cross asks us for nothing else.

✦

13

THE NAILS

It was on Good Friday that Matty died, found slumped where he had been sitting, a needle in his arm. I heard the news from a colleague at the day centre near us and wished I had been there, seen him before he was gone, or known that I'd given him a kind word the last time we met. She told me how she'd spent some time with him the previous day, listening to the story of his past, and what he had been through. She knew him so much better than we did. I listened to her sadness and compassion for him and felt inadequate, and numb. I'd never troubled to get to know him, hovering for food at our door. 'When I was hungry you gave me something to eat', Jesus said. But Matty had needed so much more than my cold charity, and now he was dead.

The public health funerals we helped arrange were simple services by necessity; one of the local clergy—Catholic or Church of England depending on how much we knew of the person's life and background—with a reading, a homily, some prayers, and a hymn. I often wrote a few words to read aloud; it seemed wrong that anyone should pass from this world anonymously, especially if there was no family to say something instead. The staff at the crematorium, and the funeral directors, were as professional as always, and other than the 9 a.m. first slot of the day, and the absence of flowers, it could have been a funeral for anyone. But Matty had never stayed with us, and I was hesitant to take a lead organizing something; in the end I found out the funeral date from the council's website and went along having had no involvement in the planning at all.

A pop song played, and the coffin was brought in, and placed on the platform to be taken away for cremation, and that was it. The staff from the day centre stood around afterwards in distress, 'One song! Is that all, to say goodbye to a life?' It was a cold dank morning, a leaden sky. I turned away from them and went to speak to his sister. She had his eyes, immaculate makeup staining as her mascara started to run under her tears, cheap and painfully new black clothes. I wondered what kind of childhood the two of them had had. 'Your brother used to come and see us sometimes for something to eat,' I said, 'I'm so sorry we didn't do more.'

I went to Mass at the place where they nailed him, one early morning; walking quickly through the narrow streets in the grey twilight before the dawn, slippery underneath with detritus from the previous day's market stalls, shutters up and footsteps echoing in the alleys as people hurried to work. The dawn in the Middle East comes quickly and by the time I reached the Holy Sepulchre it was light in the courtyard, the church full of hushed voices and people moving around in prayer. I climbed the stairs to the upper chapels, three in a row: the place of nailing, the place of crucifixion, the place of taking him down. There were only a handful of us, at six in the morning in that little chapel; a bishop celebrating, clearly a chance to come and pray before a day of leading pilgrims or some other busy work.

He came into the chapel as though walking on rose petals, and kissed the altar as one might kiss a loved one on a hospital bed. I watched him and felt myself drawn into something, a reality and presence; we were there at Mass, only more so. I found I was holding my breath. Afterwards I went into the next chapel, a few steps away, and where, under the altar, part of the rock of Calvary lay exposed. There had been a long queue of pilgrims when we'd visited earlier in the week, and I'd held back, feeling more of a tourist than a Christian coming home. This morning there was nobody about. I knelt and kissed the rock. There was a bench at the back of the chapel, partly hidden from view. I sat on it, and time passed, and after a while I found I was in tears.

And I suppose when we talk of contrition, what we mean is a sense of the reality of Calvary and the perfect generosity of Jesus who went there for us. When we pray for contrition, we are asking not to know what the nails felt like, but to know ourselves to be the ones doing the nailing. '*And let me feel it was my sin, as though no other sin there were,*' wrote one hymn writer. But there is more to it than feeling, and if we ask only for this, we are risking becoming so absorbed in ourselves that we will forget the Saviour we have followed to this place. When we pray for contrition we are praying for grace: to see the generosity of our God, and to give him all we have, even and especially the things of which we are most ashamed, in response.

When Good Friday came the next year I again covered the morning shift, an easy opportunity to allow the other staff to have some free time on a bank holiday. There was just time afterwards to hurry to church for the afternoon liturgy, arriving with the reading of the crucifixion narrative, and the veneration of the Cross after it.

The reading ended, and we formed a queue; coming forward one by one, just as the pilgrims in the Holy Sepulchre had done. I bent and kissed the little wooden feet. And stayed sitting in church for some time afterwards when the service ended, looking at the crucifix on the altar. '*Here I stay for ever viewing mercy streaming in his blood,*' wrote another Passion hymn writer, putting into words something I could not; '*While I see divine compassion floating in his languid eye.*' It seemed as though it was the first time I'd really been moved by a Good Friday service, a part of it, not just an observer.

Perhaps it was because I'd seen, now, the place where it happened. One of the things we discover in pilgrimage to the Holy Land is that we aren't really doing something we can't also do at home, because Jesus also goes to his Passion here. Perhaps the real gift of a pilgrimage is not so much the experience of going, but of helping us with what we have left behind. I loved Jerusalem, the light, the colours, the extraordinary feeling of being in the Middle East for the first time and in a place which meant so much. But I was glad to be at home that Friday afternoon, because Good Friday was also here, and the Cross and nails, and Jesus himself.

✦

14

THE VINEGAR

Tomas told us his family came from Russia, from Belarus and Ukraine; in his fifties, he had grown up in a Latvia that was part of the USSR, speaking at least three languages at home as a matter of course. We communicated in his faltering English and my three words of Lithuanian, with a great deal of reliance on hand gestures and facial expressions; I had noticed before how we hide behind fluent language, and how much more open we are with each other when we must find a way to communicate without it. He was a gentle, kind man; the whole of the staff team loved him and showed that they did, and he showed plainly his gratitude and love for us.

He drank heavily, beer and strong cider when we first knew him, but after he lost his flat and came to stay with us again after the pandemic, we found he was now drinking hand sanitizer. The bottles which had come in with Covid by the tills in every shop were a new source of alcohol to him which he had been unable to resist. He brought them home with him, concealed in his clothing; we found them in his room, one, two, three half-litre bottles at a time, 70% ethanol and empty, and Tomas unconscious on the floor. We called an ambulance, he went to hospital, came home, went into town. We found him unconscious again. I searched his room, removed full bottles he'd hidden, threw them away. I tried to reason with him: 'This is poison, don't drink it, beer is ok, this is bad.' He was embarrassed, and angry, he wanted the bottles back. I refused. He went back into town.

Then late one evening I came to check on him in his room and found him sitting on his bed, sobbing. I had known that he'd lost his wife to cancer sometime after coming to England, had nursed her, and seen her slip away from him in his arms. I thought he might be crying for that, and knelt on the floor beside him, enquiring gently. He shook his head, the tears running down. He gestured with his hands, as though batting things away from his face. I looked at the bed, and saw it was rumpled. I guessed he had been sleeping. 'Bad dream?' I asked, and he nodded, looking at me. 'Guns,' he said, miming shooting, 'my friends.' 'Where?' I asked, puzzled. I hadn't known Tomas had lived in a war zone, he had worked in cargo shipping before his increasing drinking had cost him his job and his home. He pointed at himself. 'Russia army. Bosnia.' And he began to shake.

There has been some thought that the soldiers who crucified Jesus might have been Samaritans, conscripts, given the most distasteful jobs to do among the Jewish population by a Roman authority which would have killed them in turn if they had refused orders. Or perhaps they had come with the army from Rome, for the latest job of dealing with criminals at the far end of the empire; either way, we can know that Jesus would not have been the first man they had hung up on a cross. And yet, when Jesus spoke from the Cross to say he was thirsty, one of those soldiers found a sponge, and soaked it in sour wine, and holding it up on the end of a reed pushed it into his mouth. Perhaps he was indeed a Samaritan. We might think of that other Samaritan, who stopped by the man on the Jericho road, and poured oil and wine into his wounds and bandaged them. 'Who was the neighbour?' Jesus asked the lawyer who had challenged him. 'Go and do likewise.'

Jesus said, 'I thirst.' And he would have done; he had been up all night, endured hours of pain, and was now hanging in the sun in the afternoon. But he thirsts for much more than something to drink; he thirsts for us, for us to know our need of him. The litany of the Good Friday Reproaches contrasts the ancient care of God for his people with the way we have treated him in response, and recalls the water which sprang up for Moses and the people of Israel in the wilderness: 'O my people what have I done to you? I gave you saving water from the rock, and you have given me gall and vinegar to drink.' And yet it is as vinegar, sour wine, unlovely and spoiled, that he thirsts for us.

Julian of Norwich describing her vision of the Passion called it 'the ghostly thirst that is lasting in him as long as we be in need'. We have come to the place of crucifixion, and we see Jesus there, giving his life in perfect generosity for us. And we want to give him ourselves, our perfect selves, the best that we can be, in response. It has been hard to come to this place. But how much harder it is, to give him ourselves as we really are. We are too proud, we want to give only the best. Our pride sours us still further, and Jesus sees us hesitating, and loving us all the more he says, 'I thirst.'

Perhaps Tomas might not have been able to tell me what his nightmares were about, his grief and shame for what he had seen and done, if I had not already known that he was stealing hand sanitizer, that his need for alcohol had brought him so low; no longer someone who drank cider among his Lithuanian and Russian friends and sometimes had too much, but someone in the grip of a terror he could not control. I had seen him shaking on the floor, and vomiting; I had called ambulances; perhaps it was only because he knew that I had seen all this and was still kneeling on the floor beside him, which made him able to talk. Perhaps when despite everything they do we show someone we still respect their dignity, that we help them tell us what really hurts.

Tomas died soon afterwards, his body giving up as he turned to nail polish remover as a cheap substitute when supermarkets no longer had hand sanitizer for customer use by the trolleys and the self-service tills. He had left us by that stage for other temporary accommodation, Portakabins provided by the local council with no staff on site but a security guard; I wondered if he would have lived, if he had still been with us, with people to watch and check on him, and to sit with him when he was most unwell. The last occasion he had stayed in the Portakabins he had been found unconscious by a social worker, surrounded by soiled clothes; and she'd called an ambulance, and taken home his washing, and the hospital had discharged him to us.

The local Catholic priest agreed to take a service without a fee for the public health funeral, and I was glad and grateful, because it gave us a chance to come together, and because I had heard Tomas praying aloud sometimes when he was most unwell. I wrote something for the service about our 'kind and gentle guest,' and because it was almost Christmas we sang *Silent Night*. I suppose it had been chosen for the first verse, '*Sleep in heavenly peace,*' but it seemed to say something on that winter day both of his journey and all of ours into '*the dawn of redeeming grace.*' As the light fades on Calvary, and Jesus hangs his head, our pride dies with him; and the grace which shone out from the tiny door in Bethlehem begins its work in us.

✦

15

THE SUN IN DARKNESS

It was Christmas morning, still dark, and Milee's note was on the desk when I arrived at work. I caught myself sighing, she had written me so many; long letters in uneven lettering and surprisingly good spelling, trying to explain why she'd been upset the previous day, or something which was happening with people she knew, or sometimes how she felt about staying with us. It was hard sometimes to follow up on the safeguarding disclosures these very often were, because there were so many, and they contradicted each other, and when I reported things to the police she didn't want to follow through. I'd got her a diary, so she had somewhere safe to write things if it helped her. She wrote all over it, and tore the pages out, and left them as notes for me instead. This one was shorter. 'Please come and wake me up,' it said, 'I need to tell you something.'

I was doubtful, it was still dark, and she hated early mornings. She had her dog in her room and whenever I'd had to wake her for appointments in the past I'd been met with snarling, barking and then cursing from Milee as she shouted to the dog to be quiet; it was a job I tried to avoid if I could. I called her name cautiously outside her door. The dog whimpered a little. A muffled voice said 'Come in,' so I did, and found her sitting on her bed. The dog came and licked me and lay down. I sat on the floor beside them.

Milee had often talked about her father. He'd stayed with us himself, some years before; monosyllabic with us and muttering to himself, he was a strange man and hard to get to know. He would still acknowledge me in the street, mostly, if I said hello to him first. I always had the impression he had spotted me before I saw him. She had seen him in town the previous day, she had been sitting begging for money for crack, a good day for 'drops' of cash on her blanket, from shoppers out on Christmas Eve. Her father had come by, she said, and asked if she'd like to come home with him for a bit because it was Christmas. He'd given her a £20 note, and she'd thought it was a Christmas present. Then he had made clear he was buying her services like the other clients she had, and he'd raped her in the flat. Outside I could hear the birds begin singing, it was a mild morning, a grey light had begun to creep into the room. The dog whimpered again. 'Was it the first time,' I asked, finding something to say. 'No,' she said, 'he got me pregnant. This baby, and the one last summer that I lost.' We think, sometimes, that we must have seen the worst. And then we discover that the darkness is so much darker than we had thought.

The darkness which the Gospels tell us 'covered the whole land' for three hours that Friday afternoon could not simply have been a solar eclipse; not only because of the length of time involved, but also by the fact that a solar eclipse occurs during a new moon, whereas the Friday was the eve of the Passover, and the moon was full. We must find another way to understand it, the darkness which turned everything on that spring day to night, as Jesus hung in agony on the Cross, and cried out 'My God why have you forsaken me?' and in that desolation died alone in the dark.

The experience for anyone in Jerusalem that day must have been terrifying. We read not only of the darkness, but of the earthquake, the bodies released from their tombs, an extraordinary account which at the very least tells us that people that day encountered something they had never experienced before.

The rock of Calvary which we kneel to kiss is cracked. And we might understand all this also as a way of describing a mystery greater even than the darkness which expresses it, that Jesus knew what it is to feel separated from God, and in that moment is closest to us.

The truth is that we are never forsaken by God, who counts the hairs of our heads and is closer than our own breath. Our experience however can be the opposite, when pain or grief, depression, fear, a faltering faith, or simply the absorbing nature of our own sin can make God seem very far away, so far that we may feel there is nothing there at all. Jesus knew what this felt like, and we can look into the darkness of that Friday afternoon and know that in sharing our experience so completely Jesus has made separation into intimacy, darkness into light. 'My God,' he cries across the void, not only God, but *my* God, who knows everything about me. And from that moment we are no longer alone.

✦

I drove Milee to the city two days later, for the first appointment after the Christmas bank holidays, arranged by the police detective before what they called the 'forensic window' closed. The place was intended to look as anonymous as possible, the parking at the back away from the street. Milee took one look at the nurse and refused to go into the clinical room. 'I'm pregnant, you can't use that, it's not safe, it will give me a miscarriage.' The nurse explained the procedure again. It was 27 December, and I thought of the Evangelist whose feast it was, 'the Word was made flesh and dwelt among us'. How agonizing this existence in the flesh could be. They gave her some swabs, and told her to do her best in the toilet. My phone began to ring and I went out into the car park while they conferred.

It was the hospital, back in town. Rachel, who had suffered with cancer and liver failure, who I'd been to see so often with

Patrick and once on my own, had died half an hour before. I
called my colleagues, and asked them to tell him. The winter sun
was bright in the cold December air, the detective and the nurse
were still conferring, Milee was still in the toilet, perhaps trying
to swab her genitals, or perhaps afraid to provide any evidence
at all. There is a shock when we hear of a death, no matter how
unwell the person has been; a sudden void of someone who was
here, and now has gone. We can get used to seeing people dying.
But none of us knows what it is to be dead, or where a person is
now, when they have been with us, and suddenly they are not.

Milee was silent on the way home, and I was too, thinking of
Rachel, and her 'infamous reputation,' as the police officer was
to write to me later that day, 'A young life gone too soon. How
sad.' We stopped for petrol and I bought Milee a Coke, and a
Creme Egg, because eggs were her invariable breakfast and because it seemed such a bizarre thing to find Easter eggs for sale
on 27 December. She took it and smiled, the first time since
Christmas Eve. It melted in her pocket and we arrived back at
the house to find the car seat covered in chocolate. I told her not
to worry, it needed cleaning anyway, and boiled her some real
eggs for lunch. I went upstairs to see Patrick. Perhaps sometimes
there is nothing we can do but walk on together in the dark and,
in one another's company, find some reminder that our grief has
already been shared.

✦

16

THE SPEAR

Marta's liver began to fail, and as it did so her body became less and less able to cope. She drank less, but the pain and difficulties of day-to-day living began to make her cranky sometimes. She suffered seizures, and needed help with her medication, and a carer began to come daily to make sure she was taking what she should. She refused the carers' offer of assistance with washing and dressing vehemently but she let Milee help her, surprisingly gentle and efficient as she was; though sometimes we thought a bottle of vodka in the shower might have been involved. And she had a clinic at the hospital every fortnight, to drain the fluid in her abdomen. We used to tell her to catch the bus, until the hospital called to say they would no longer treat her unless one of our staff came with her.

I was one of only a couple of staff with a car insured for work, so I took on the task of taking Marta to her appointments. She hated going, and because she hated being there she hated to wait; it became clear why I'd been asked to come along. And she would sit in a chair, a tube would be inserted through her abdomen into her stomach, with a bag, and over three or four hours the fluid which bloated her and left her so short of breath would slowly drip out. I couldn't stay for it all and would leave her there, asking the nurse to call a taxi when it was time to come home. Later she would reappear, trying to tell us how it had been, 'Six litres Lucy, big problem!' and wanting snacks for dinner.

Then one morning I found her in the dining room, her hand over her side, panting and beckoning. 'Let me see,' I said, thinking that perhaps the dressing had come loose, or some other complication. She lifted her hand, and I saw that the dressing was soaked in blood. I steered her into the first-aid room, coaxing and reassuring, gloves on, dressings out, and started to peel off the tapes. Then I clapped my hand over her side and began to press as hard as I could, reaching for my phone with the other hand. The blood was pouring out through my fingers, and Marta slumped down on a chair.

✦

The steps down from the Calvary chapel are cut from red stone, a reminder of the blood and water which came out from the side of Jesus when the soldier thrust in the spear. We descend from Calvary that way, and there is no other, because the way we came up is full of people following behind: there is one way to the Cross, and one way leading on. The stairs are narrow, and worn; I thought how many feet had come that way before.

We sometimes hear the blood and water described in sacramental terms as the water of baptism and the wine of the Eucharist, the pouring out of grace which washes us when we first become Christians, and again and again each time we come for communion. In that sense the sacramental life of the Church was born at this moment, as blood and water were poured out from the dead Christ on the Cross. But seeing someone bleeding, really bleeding, so that it cannot be stopped, is shocking; a sign not of life but of death, a thing which should be hidden now hideously in view, red, messy, something gone terribly wrong. It is easy to say we have been washed in his blood, much less so to comprehend the physical reality of what this means. And then we might reflect that being washed is something done to us, not something we do with our own action; like a small child must be washed, or a sick person who cannot manage for themselves.

And we might become dirty again another time, or in another way, but that which has been washed off has gone for good.

This, then, is what happens with the things we write on the title of the Cross. We are washed, like children, or sick people, because sick children are what we are, and the things which it cost us to bring here, and cost him so much more, are washed away and gone. The blood of Jesus, flowing from a broken heart, cleanses and heals us, and the thrust of the spear in his side is itself an answer to our feeble prayers for contrition. The heart of our God longs to give us everything, and our response of love begins here at the foot of the Cross, as we see his wounds for what they are, and begin to allow grace and mercy to wash over us.

Marta was taken from the local hospital to a bigger one with a specialist ward, and from there to the isolation ward on the top floor, with a view far over the fields. The tuberculosis which a test on the general ward had picked up was thought to be in her blood rather than her lungs, and visits were allowed, and for three months that summer I was her only visitor, coming once a week with any letters she'd received, and messages from friends, and a chance to ask a nurse or doctor how she was coming along. Marta lay quietly in her room, day by day and week by week. The ward staff were amazed at her patience, 'She never reads, or watches TV.' Then one Sunday I pointed out the view to her, the wheat turned golden in the afternoon sun, the woods in the distance, and a combine harvester making its way up and down. She showed no interest, and seemed not to know what I meant. I realized that whatever she knew beyond the window was not the wheat, nor the harvesting or the trees, because she could no longer see them.

She was turned down by the liver transplant consultant, 'It's a waste, she'll go back to the same friends and the same situation being homeless, she'll only start drinking again,' and transferred her back to the local hospital. My work grew busier, and I hoped her friends were visiting; I put it off from one week to the next, absorbed in money worries, the lack of funding from the local council, and postponing our autumn reopening of the house because we could not pay the staff to run it. There came a Friday when I had almost resolved to give up, and sick at heart and too tired to face an evening of emails I thought I might as well call in at the hospital.

Marta welcomed me joyfully, 'Lucita, Lucita'! and patted the bed beside her. I fetched a chair, and noticed the nurses smiling; clearly she was no longer in need of a staff escort to cope with hospital here. She pulled a newspaper cutting from under her pillow, and smoothed it out carefully. It was from the local free paper that morning; the headline referred to our financial crisis, and the text was a fair summary of everything which had gone wrong in the last few weeks. In the middle was a large picture of the house, red roof, green door, garden, an old image they'd had on file. 'Lucita!' she said again, and kissed the picture happily. She could not read the newsprint; she had never read letters in English, even when she could see well. But she recognized the picture, and for her it was a picture of home, of safety and of being loved; all the misery and failure which the text contained meant nothing, any more than the time she had had to wait to see me. I found a wheelchair and took her out into the corridors; we came back soon, because she was tired. I left her with the nurses, settling for the night, and next morning I began to pray for help to begin our work once more.

✦

17

The Ladder

Stephen's son Jacob died less than three months after bringing his father to us. The police arrived late one evening, not an unusual event, but sat down with Stephen, holding their hats, and told him that Jacob's body had been found that evening. And during the next few days a trickle of visitors came to the door, asking for him, asking us to pass on condolences; cocaine and heroin addicts, alcoholics, people sleeping rough, others who seemed to be staying anywhere they could with friends. They came with dignity, and respect; we underestimate sometimes what people are still capable of, when their lives in other ways are filled with chaos.

It was Stephen's daughter, Jacob's younger sister, together with her grandparents, who arranged the funeral. Stephen's wife had died when the children were at primary school, his drinking and drug use escalated, he could no longer work to pay the rent, and the family had moved in with his parents. He loved his children, but he could not be a father to them; when he eventually approached the funeral director to ask about planning a service for Jacob, he found that Stacey had organized everything and her grandparents had paid. 'We tried to contact him,' said the funeral director, 'but he didn't answer his phone and we had to go with the next of kin we could find.'

He had no suit for the funeral day, but he was clean, and sober, and although he sobbed through the two pop songs Stacey had chosen—the ones she remembered from her mother's funeral—he was able to stay until the end. I listened to the civil celebrant telling stories from Jacob's childhood and thought how much was left unsaid: the pain, the homelessness which had been the end of his life. I remembered the autumn evening they had appeared on our doorstep, and how Jacob had insisted his father take the room, and then gone to stay with friends, taking drugs, taking such terrible risks. I felt sick of funerals, and angry at the lack of honesty in them. 'Sleep tight Jacob, you have your angel wings,' said the celebrant, and I winced and looked at Stephen, who was crying too hard to hear. I gave Stephen's girl-friend a lift home, she had wanted to borrow my black shoes on the way there, having come in trainers by mistake. 'It was a lovely funeral,' she said. I'd had enough. 'Where can I drop you?' I answered.

In the fourth century the empress Helena, mother of Constantine, whose conversion to Christianity must have felt like an extraordinary answer to prayer to those who had known the persecutions of his predecessors, set out from Rome in her late seventies to travel to Jerusalem and search for the holy places of her faith. The three crosses came to light buried under the temple of Venus which St Jerome tells us had been built over Calvary, an act intended as desecration by the emperor Hadrian but which served to mark for future generations the place which had known true Love. We're told that the Cross of Christ was identified from the other two by the healing of a patient at the point of death who touched it to her skin, but however they managed it the place is marked now by a chapel under the cracked rock of Calvary, where Adam is believed to have been buried. The fragments of the true Cross which were found in the earth were taken from there first to Stavrovouni Monastery in Cyprus, lovely among the olive trees on a mountain by the sea and where a piece was given in thanksgiving after a storm on the way home, and then to the new basilica of Santa Croce in Rome, where the empress died shortly after.

John Climacus on Mount Sinai in the seventh century, and Walter Hilton in the English Midlands in the fourteenth, were to write of the 'ladder of ascent' or 'ladder of perfection' by which souls may climb to heaven, each step or rung representing a truth to be grasped, a change of heart, or a challenge overcome by grace. And perhaps we might understand such an image best by thinking of the ladder by which the body of Jesus was taken down from the Cross, a hard and physically awkward job in the twilight of Good Friday, as our own same ladder of burdens which we must overcome if we are to climb back to God. We might find then that the things we have tried hardest to bury in the earth at the foot of it, our pride and self-will, the sins we are most reluctant to name, are the things which will help us most to grow in holiness: and will become the steps of the ladder which Jacob saw in his dream, reaching from earth to heaven and with angels coming up and down to help us on the way.

Or we might picture ourselves at Mass, showing up on time, preparing our thoughts, waiting patiently, coming up for communion. We think, perhaps, that this coming up to present ourselves is something which, with a little organization and discipline, we have achieved ourselves. We forget that this encounter is not our work but God's, who comes down from the altar to us just as he did on the ladder of Calvary on that Friday afternoon. We see the bread and chalice lifted up as bread and wine, and down as the body and blood of Jesus who has endured everything to make this descent to us. We receive the gift of his perfect generosity, and so are helped to give him, step by step, our own.

✦

Some weeks later I was cleaning Stephen's room when, in a moment of carelessness, I took my eyes off my hands and an uncapped needle went through the protective glove. I flushed the wound under the tap and took myself to A&E, thankful that whatever happened it had at least happened to me and not to one of the rest of the team. I was there some hours and given various tests as well as a vaccination for hepatitis and, because Stephen's girlfriend was known to be a sex worker, I was also started on a month's treatment against HIV. 'It might make you a bit sick,' they said, which indeed turned out to be the case.

It was nearly six when I returned, and Stephen had come back from wherever he had spent the day, and was crying in the dining room, with one of my colleagues sitting with him. He stumbled up from his chair when he saw me and came limping over, tears running down his face. He was so sorry, he said, it was all his fault, they'd told him what had happened and how I'd had to go to hospital and he was so sorry, I'd been so good to him, and he had done this to me. I was astonished; Stephen's untidiness and his drug use were so much a part of caring for him that it had never occurred to me to blame him. I thought of using the moment to suggest Stephen kept his room tidier, but it didn't seem right to say it; after all, I knew well enough to watch what I was doing while I worked. It is a strange thing to receive such a heartfelt apology for something for which one feels no anger; more often we find that the emotion is ours, distress or anger, and the other person's apology seems inadequate or never comes at all.

Perhaps Stephen learned something from the experience. But the month of antiretroviral drugs which followed, the twice-daily remembering to take them as much as the sickness they involved, was in itself a lesson for me; that we cannot do this work unless we are prepared to share in the pain of those we help, not only in their present but also in the trauma of their past. Stephen used needles for a reason, because heroin and its synthetic substitutes made him forget his pain; what he needed most from us was that we should not forget it too. We use so many things to help us forget the pain of what we have suffered, and of what we have made others suffer. Our desperate need is that our God will find us even in the worst of these things, and will come down the ladder of ascent to us.

✦

18

THE MYRRH

Stephen's last stay in hospital was not on that May afternoon when I had gone with him in the ambulance, sirens blaring, and tried to help the doctor in critical care. It was a damp autumn day the following year when his mother called me, and I had seen him a couple of weeks before, crouched on the pavement, searching through a broken carrier bag while the paraphernalia of drug use spilled onto the tarmac. He had been chased by kids, he said, they would beat him up, and I walked him to the railway station to catch a train to the flat which was, at last, his home. 'Stephen is in hospital,' said his mother, 'he's been unconscious, maybe you could go and see him.' I went that evening, and cycling through the dark streets among the autumn leaves I thought again of the night he had first agreed to stay with us, two years ago almost to the day.

He lay in a side room of the ward, his eyes were closed, and his mother was at the side of the bed. She left us for a while and I took his swollen hand carefully, saying his name. He opened his eyes a little, unfocused, and began to talk, painfully, with odd absences between. I asked him how he felt. 'I'm scared Luce, I'm scared of the devil,' and I was surprised, because he always called me 'miss' out of habit formed in prison, or 'mate' when he was in a more expansive mood. Stephen's ideas of religion had always seemed to me a bit eclectic—his only contribution to his son's funeral plan had been to visit the funeral parlour the day before and put pennies on his eyes 'To pay the boatman, you know, make sure he gets there safe'; he shared one of my colleague's tastes in Christian rock music but would talk at length about a kingdom under the earth which seemed to be something to do with the apocryphal Gospels, or possibly Mormonism. I had generally tried to get him off the subject.

The devil, however, was easier to grasp. 'This is a place of God, not the devil,' I said firmly, 'look how many people are here to help you and care about you. Look at how much your mother loves you, she has been to see you every day since you came here.' He began to cry. 'I've done a lot of things wrong Luce,' which was undoubtedly true but I was inadequate to the task of helping him. 'Yes,' I said, trying to sound as matter of fact as though we were back at the dining table discussing his untidy room, 'we all do. Think about God, not the devil, you are loved and you will be ok.' His eyes had lost focus again and I went to find his mother, 'Come again soon,' she said. The various machines and tubes attached to Stephen continued their work of fluids and drips, and I left them together, she again sitting by his bed.

✦

The anointing stone where the body of Jesus was laid is just inside the entrance to the Church of the Holy Sepulchre, near the steps to Calvary; a marble slab, pinky-yellow and smooth, with lamps hanging above. You can kneel there among the pilgrims, and bend to kiss it, and it smells richly sweet, because so much scented oil has been rubbed into it for so many years. I saw several Orthodox women doing just that and thought of Mary of Bethany with the alabaster jar and her long hair, and envied their lack of self-consciousness.

And yet we are given, day by day, an opportunity to anoint the body of Jesus, just as in that scene at supper on the eve of Palm Sunday, or like those pilgrims who honour him by anointing the stone. The pound of pure nard asked from us at the foot of the Cross is the gift of our obedience, the renunciation of our own wills, which in our frailty we can give only if we ask for it first as a tremendous gift of grace, and which like Mary's gift comes at a huge cost—'why was this perfume not sold for three hundred denarii and given to the poor'. And for myself I have always found the idea a terrifying one: we are asked to obey, which means to trust God completely, and to say 'Thy will be done' without worrying what will happen next.

But the very fact that this final anointing takes place by the rock of Calvary is also a help to understanding what obedience will mean for us. Mary and John watched from where we are standing, and heard Jesus say to them 'Behold your mother,' and 'Behold your son': giving them both a task and vocation for life, and also the gifts of security and consolation which they needed most. The work we will be given in response to our obedience will equally be the request of one who loves us dearly, and so can only be for our good. And perhaps the scene with the pound of pure nard is a warning to us, as well as a challenge, because Mary of Bethany chose that moment, six days before he died, to anoint Jesus with the most precious thing she had, 'she has been keeping it for the day she prepares for my burial.' Perhaps she was afraid she might not have another chance. The myrrh and sweet spices of our obedience are not asked in the future, when we have done all the other things we want to do, and feel ready. We are asked to give them now.

My last visit to Stephen was a few days later, and I found him on a different ward because he had been difficult with the nurses on the other ward, and they had said they could not look after him. I was encouraged by the news; if Stephen was well enough to swear at people, he must be getting better. The nurse on the reception desk looked at me doubtfully and asked me to wait while he went and spoke to Stephen. He reappeared in a few minutes and said I could go in.

Stephen on his new bed seemed twice the size of when I'd last seen him, his body swollen with infection and every limb tight and red. His face was bleak with pain. 'My balls are the size of coconuts mate, it effing hurts,' he said, wincing as he tried to move in bed. 'Yes I'm sure, how are you feeling in yourself?' I said. We talked about his mother's visits, and if his daughter had been to see him, Stacey who had arranged her brother's funeral. Not yet. The nurse came in after a while and Stephen introduced me, 'My support worker, she's bloody good.' 'Stephen stayed with us about six months,' I said, embarrassed and hoping the nurse would understand from this what I didn't want to shame Stephen by saying. I saw the nurse's expression change to respect and gathered that Stephen in hospital must have been very difficult indeed. We went out for some air, the nurse pushing the plus-size wheelchair, and I was grateful, because I would have struggled to do it. I said goodbye under the smoking shelter, and Stephen thanked me for coming, and a couple of days afterwards his mother called to tell me he had gone. 'Did Stacey see him?' 'Yes she did.'

Nicodemus brought more than fifty pounds of myrrh and aloes when he came to help Joseph of Arimathea prepare Jesus for burial, an enormous quantity, and we might picture them by the anointing stone—or one very like it—cleaning the wounds as Friday afternoon turned to evening, preparing the body until the sweat and blood of the last twenty four hours was wiped away and every part of him smelled sweet. They did for him in that sense what Jesus does for each of us, not only because if we believe in the resurrection of the body we know that in some way that which has decayed will be made new, but also because he takes the sickness and sweat of our souls and prepares us in a final act of grace for what is to come. We die so hideously sometimes, and with so much sin clinging to us. His sweat and blood are our myrrh and aloes, and as he is prepared for the grave, so we are prepared for heaven.

19

THE SHROUD

Marta, when she came back from the city TB ward, was in and out of the local hospital, and I visited generally once a week, or sometimes instead in her new home. The tiny downstairs flat was a tremendous pride to her and she kept it beautifully, her collections of ornaments, and bath bubbles, and trainers, all neatly arranged. Her medication always seemed rather more confused and I would glance through the book her carers had left, glad that someone was keeping a record of what she had taken or not. I took her a box of chocolates, and the fruit that she liked, on Christmas Day after I'd finished on shift. Sometimes Milee would come with me to the hospital, and if I had thought about it I would have seen then how ill Marta really was, because the things I had grown accustomed to made Milee so silent, and she would cry on the way home. They loved each other but Marta was candid enough about Milee in her absence—'Milee narcotics? Bah! No good!'

Then one Saturday morning at the beginning of February Marta called me from hospital, very distressed. I understood so little of what she was saying that in the end I said I would come and see her that afternoon, and hung up. And I don't know what I expected, some misunderstanding with the nurses perhaps, but I came into the ward, and saw her sitting up in bed, and her face was gaunt and yellow, and her mouth black where she had bitten her lips and they had bled, and her eyes were wide and desperate, and something about her had changed. I found myself hurrying across the ward, and kneeling by her bed, and she took hold of my hand and poured out her distress in a flood of Lithuanian and Russian of which I understood only one word, 'Lucita!' She had brought her bottle of morphine to hospital unknown to the staff, and taken it all in one go that morning. The hospital had her on one-to-one observation thinking it had been a suicide attempt. I was doubtful, and Marta could not tell us what she had been intending, and the nurse who spoke Lithuanian was not due until the evening.

I left her after a while, unable to calm her, and wanting to get on with the day. I finished late at work, setting the alarm for a busy Sunday ahead. The phone rang at 1 am, it was the hospital, Marta was getting worse, they thought I ought to know. I woke up enough to say I would be there the next afternoon, thank you for telling me. I went back to sleep. The phone rang again at half past one. It was the doctor this time. Marta was really very ill indeed. Again I said I would be there in the afternoon. And at midday next day I picked up my phone after Mass to find a voicemail left sometime during communion, ten minutes before. It was the doctor, and Marta was dead.

The shroud which so famously is kept in Turin has a copy in Rome, next to the chapel in Santa Croce where the other relics of the Passion are displayed, and which anyone can visit and see. It shows very plainly the wounds of the body it is supposed to have wrapped, and perhaps it is indeed the burial cloth of Jesus, or perhaps it is a work of medieval devotion, and perhaps on one level it doesn't really matter. It helps us in so far as it enables us to see the wounds, and to know that this is what is meant by dying to ourselves, because looking at his wounds is the best help we have to thinking no longer of our own. *'His dying crimson, like a robe, spreads o'er his body on the tree; then am I dead*

to all the world, and all the world is dead to me.' The linen cloth was brought by Joseph of Arimathea, say all four Gospels. Perhaps he had been keeping it for himself, just as he offered the use of his own tomb.

There are times when the reality of our sin dawns upon us slowly, as we allow ourselves to be open to grace. There are times when grace seems to intervene in spite of ourselves, miraculous times, when something we had not thought we could do becomes suddenly possible, or we find we can forgive someone, or we can apologize for something we have refused to before. And then there are times when this visit of the Holy Spirit is something like a waking up in the dark, and we realize we had been dreaming in a nightmare of our self-absorption, and it is still night, and we lie helpless in this cold new consciousness of ourselves waiting for the morning. We forget Peter, who went out from the high priest's courtyard before the dawn and wept; and how the nightmare must have seemed to him an eternity, between that hour and the dawn of Easter day. We forget the church of Gallicantu, and the painting in its central place over the altar. And we forget what happened when Peter tried to put it all from his mind and go back to work, only to see his Lord in the early morning, with mercy such as he had never before understood it, standing on the lake shore.

I cried bitterly when the doctor rang. I knew how much Marta would have wanted me there when she was dying, would have been asking for me; I had seen how frightened she was, and the empty bottle of morphine told me how much she was in pain. I cried for what I had not done, for an opportunity I could never have back; and in bewilderment, because despite the loss of so many people I had cared for I still did not know how to pray for the dead. And I became a professional again, I called the hospital, the body would be on the ward until three o'clock they said, then they would need the bed. I drove to work, picked up a colleague, and we went on to the hospital together.

She lay as if sleeping, smiling a little, her eyes were closed. We sat a while, and then I drew the sheet up over her face, and we came away. We see hospital staff most often when they are caring for the living, rushed off their feet as often as not, and not always with as much time as we would like for us. We forget that they care for us also when we die, and the work they do then, when we cannot appreciate it, and when there is no-one else to do it. Marta when we saw her was not lying as she had been when she died. Someone had taken out the catheters and the drain in her side, had lifted her, and changed the sheets for us to come and see her, and laid her gently out in bed.

And yet it is not only our burial cloth which enfolds Jesus, but also his which enfolds us; a place of perfect safety where, hidden in his wounds, we do not have to be afraid of anything, not even of ourselves. We are in a place where everything is known and where we cannot be threatened by self and its desires, because here we are with God. '*Within thy wounds hide me,*' says a famous fourteenth century prayer, written perhaps around the time that the Shroud was first discovered, '*suffer me not to be separated from thee.*' And we are hidden in his five wounds, we die to ourselves, whenever we come to be reconciled with God. Perhaps we come preoccupied with the list we have made beforehand of our own wounds needing to be healed. Perhaps we might be thinking of the perfect generosity of the Passion, and come wanting to be generous with what we have done. But more than anything we come here to die, and to find that contrition is not some impossible exercise in feeling sorry enough, but simply to be in the wounds of Jesus and to want nothing else.

✦

20

THE TOMB

There is a tradition in Russian Orthodoxy for prayers to be said on the third day after a person has died, and on the ninth, and on the fortieth; a ritual and sequence for grieving, and for commending a soul to God. Arranging a funeral for Marta, however, turned out to be an unexpectedly difficult task, as she had died in hospital without family or a plan to pay for one, and the hospital chaplaincy in such circumstances would usually arrange to take a simple service at the crem. The Orthodox do not cremate their dead, and I had to argue hard for the hospital to pay for a burial. Their local priest could not have been kinder or more generous with his time, and I tried to plan the logistics, which was complicated as Marta had so many friends wanting to come. Everything had to be communicated through the two who spoke some English, and they did not always tell me the same thing, and then the chapel at the funeral directors was very small, and we all needed to be transported to the burial ground afterwards. And so many of my colleagues wanted to go too, and the nurses who had cared for her needed to be told of the arrangements, and Milee, who would need looking after, and who was afraid to come.

It was a still grey day at the beginning of March when we gathered. They had brought flowers, the coffin and the chapel were filled with them, and the priest chanted on, and some of Marta's friends stood listening and weeping through it all, and others came in and out, bringing more flowers, going out for a

cigarette. One left his can of cider respectfully on the funeral parlour urn of artificial plants in the hall, before going in. His friend
took it off and held it discreetly behind his back, grimacing at
me, 'What's he like.' We sorted ourselves into cars, and went up
to the burial ground.

It was the council municipal cemetery, large and neat with
paths and shining marble monuments, with taps and water bottles and ornaments, and little hedges, and dark trees at one end.
We walked with the hearse, a long line of us, past all the other
rows of graves to the top of the field. We stood around, and there
was incense, and holy water, and more singing, and then it was
over, and we took the flowers which had filled the chapel, and
dropped them into the grave on top of the coffin, pink roses, yellow, and red, single carnations done up beautifully in ribbons;
they were gifts from people who had very little, some of them
came to our door from time to time asking for something to eat.
The sun came out suddenly in a late afternoon glory, gold on
the people, the drifting incense and the flowers, and I felt it
warm on my face.

It was early on a Sunday morning when I visited the Holy
Sepulchre itself, a little building under the dome of the church,
and inside an antechamber with an altar, and beyond that an
inner chamber, with a ledge banked up with roses and lilies.
The place was warm and sweet with their perfume. 'There was
a garden at the place where they crucified him', and it should
not surprise us that excavations very recently in the ground
nearby have found traces of olives and vines in the soil. There
was a garden, and a tomb among the olive trees, and we have
come back to where we began: 'for the sake of you, who left a
garden, I was betrayed in a garden, and crucified in a garden',
says Christ to Adam in the old Greek homily which is read in
church during the Office of Readings on Holy Saturday.

And it is here in the silence of Holy Saturday, the deepest mystery of our faith, that we must leave our grief and pain with God. We say that Christ harrowed hell that day, and we might think of the icons which show him armed with the Cross at the door of hell, leading Adam out. We might think of that descent also as the journey of our Lord to the very darkest places of our souls, to the hells we have fallen into, or created for ourselves. He comes to look for us, waking from our dreams and nightmares, and he takes us by the hand in the dark. We cannot know, in this life, what lies beyond the grave. But we can know what it is to be visited by grace, and to be taken by the hand, and led out into the light.

The place where Mary of Magdala met her Lord is marked on the church floor not far from the tomb, with an altar, and candles, a place where people kneel and kiss the marble floor. Teresa of Ávila in describing the soul's progress in the life of prayer writes of a garden which God plants and prepares, and which we must allow him to tend, and we might take the thought further and reflect that one day we will meet our God, like Mary, in a garden, the garden both of Paradise and of our souls. We will meet him then inasmuch as we allow him to be a gardener now, in the hard labour of digging, the painful lessons of weeding and pruning, and the long work of watering. Our tears in the night of Good Friday are only a beginning. Our real growth as Christians begins on Easter morning, when our penitence knows what the cost of love has been, and the empty tomb is filled with the flowers which grace has grown, and the wounded hands of Jesus show us the true nature of what has been forgiven.

✦

We planted a rose garden for them all, for Rachel and Jacob, Jamie and Stephen, Matty and Tomas and Marta and the others. Their names are written on the garden wall, a reminder that despite the chaos and pain of their lives they are precious to God, and with a simple inscription: 'In my Father's house are many rooms.' Some of the people who helped us plant the first roses have since been added themselves. I liked to think that the garden honoured the living, also, and might be a help to the people we cared for; in showing them that they would not be forgotten, in a world where life could be taken by sickness, or a hit of contaminated drugs, and death seemed sometimes very close.

On the first anniversary after Marta died I went back to where she had been buried, to the little mound of rough grass where her friends had left candle stubs and came sometimes to pray. I took a trowel and planted snowdrops in the green in the scrubby wet earth, that they might flower at that time each year; it was a damp grey day, muddy under my knees, and cold on my hands. I dug for a while, and thought how the rain would help the plants to root well, and I wondered if the spotless white of their flowers would spread, and if the other graves would soon have snowdrops too. I remembered the hospital bed, and the calls in the night. And the memory of those denials was no longer a pit of my own self-pity, but a precious help in following the Lord, because grief is part of the glory of Easter, and because since Adam it has been in our sin that we have been found by God.

'He is not here, he is risen', said the angel at the tomb. I had thought of those words in the Holy Sepulchre, in the inner chamber among the flowers; perhaps when we do not know how to pray for the dead, or for ourselves, we might simply say this. For Christians it is always Easter morning. And the Lord finds us here, kneeling on the earth on a cold winter's day, and says to us also, 'Awake O sleeper and rise from the dead, and Christ will give you light.'

✦

NOTES

Page 53: '*And let me feel it was my sin, as though no other sin there were*', F. W. Faber, from the hymn 'My God, my God, and can it be'; '*Here I stay for ever viewing mercy streaming in his blood*' and '*while I see divine compassion floating in his languid eye*', Walter Shirley, from the hymn 'Sweet The Moments, Rich in Blessing'.

Page 57: 'the ghostly thirst that is lasting in him as long as we be in need', Julian of Norwich, *Revelations of Divine Love*, chapter xxxi.

Pages 77–8: '*His dying crimson, like a robe ...*', Isaac Watts, from the hymn 'When I Survey the Wondrous Cross'.

Page 79: '*Within thy wounds hide me, suffer me not to be separated from thee*', from the prayer 'Anima Christi', possibly written by Pope John XXII, and cited by St Ignatius of Loyola.

SLG PRESS PUBLICATIONS

www.slgpress.co.uk

The Sisters of the Love of God is an Anglican community of women religious living a contemplative monastic life.

To learn more about the Community and the Convent of the Incarnation at Fairacres, Oxford, see our website www.slg.org.uk.

As well as supporting those seeking to follow a vocation to the monastic life, the Community has a number of forms of association for those who feel drawn to share in the Sisters' life of prayer: Fellowship of the Love of God, Companions, Priests Associate and Oblate Sisters.

For more information email sisters@slg.org.uk or write to The Reverend Mother, Convent of the Incarnation, Parker Street, Oxford, OX4 1TB, UK.